HOME, SWEET HOME
THE WARTIME LETTERS OF

Sgt Pilot Bob Kimberley Illustrated by Ken Kimberley

HOME, SWEET HOME

THE WARTIME LETTERS OF

Sgt Pilot Bob Kimberley   Illustrated by Ken Kimberley

Webb & Bower

MICHAEL JOSEPH

To mum
with love

First published in Great Britain 1989 by
Webb & Bower (Publishers) Limited
5 Cathedral Close, Exeter, Devon EX1 1EZ
in association with Michael Joseph Limited
27 Wright's Lane, London W8 5TZ

Penguin Books Ltd, Registered Offices: Harmondsworth, Middlesex, England
Penguin Books Australia Ltd, Ringwood, Victoria, Australia
Penguin Books Canada Ltd, 2801 John Street, Markham, Ontario, Canada L3R 1D4
Penguin Books (NZ) Ltd, 182–190 Wairau Road, Auckland 10, New Zealand

Designed by Vic Giolitto

Production by Nick Facer/Rob Kendrew

Text and illustrations Copyright © 1989 Ken Kimberley

British Library Cataloguing in Publication Data

Kimberley, A.J. (Albert James), *1921–1944*
    Home sweet home:the wartime letters of Sgt.
    Pilot A.J. Kimberley
    1. World War 2. Air operations by Great
    Britain, Royal Air Force, Fighter
    aeroplanes. Pilots – Biographies
    I. Title
    940.54'4941'0924

ISBN 0-86350-314-4

Typeset in Great Britain by P&M Typesetting Limited, Exeter, Devon

Colour reproduction by Peninsular Repro Service Limited, Exeter, Devon

Printed and bound in Hong Kong

CONTENTS

Never mind kid, we'll just have to get the old bikes out again!

INTRODUCTION

Albert James 'Bob' Kimberley was born in Plaistow, London E13 on 17th January 1921. 'Bob' quickly became preferable to 'Bert'. His early schooldays were spent at Balaam Street School where he, like his family before him, received a solid education. The teachers were wonderful, caring people – Tom Lethaby, 'Jock' Hannah and Len Murray taught all the basics and Old Solly did his best with art. Each one was much respected and held in the highest esteem by the pupils. In time-honoured fashion, Bob would walk down Balaam Street, taking the short cut through the park, squeeze through the gap in the fence and into school to begin the day's lessons.

Bob Kimberley after being awarded his wings – Canada, spring 1943.

It soon became apparent that Bob Kimberley was a bright pupil. He won a much-prized scholarship to the comparatively new Plaistow Secondary School which, at that time, was the best of its type in east London. He excelled at art and by the time he matriculated he was also well tutored in French, German and Latin. He had also built up an impressive portfolio of art work and it was not long before he realized an early ambition. His work impressed John Dickinson of Tottenham and he was offered a position in the Commercial Art Department.

Bob Kimberley was a keen cyclist and most weekends he and his brother Ken would head for the north Essex countryside – he was extremely proud of his special Claud Butler bike, with its hand-built frame, three-speed gears and dropped racing handlebars.

Learning to drive was a top priority and passing the comparitively new driving test was a challenge which had to be overcome. Bob Kimberley passed – one of the youngest successful first-time applicants in Plaistow – and the reward was a shining blue Hillman Minx, a four-door saloon with a sliding sun-roof. He spent considerably more time polishing his pride and joy than sitting behind the wheel.

When the Second World War broke out, Bob's younger brother Ken was evacuated to relatives in Staffordshire. Bob drove his brother to safer surroundings, but on the way the car suffered a slight knock – Hitler and the war were quickly forgotten! The dent was pushed out and the car returned to its pristine condition – Bob did not want to meet his only rich uncle with his most valuable possession showing signs of wear and tear.

When the Blitz came to Balaam Street it claimed the Kimberley home and the cherished Hillman Minx – so, for Bob, it was back to the Claud Butler bicycle.

Bob's father died in 1927 and his mother had remarried. The family moved to Hornchurch in Essex (a long-standing ambition for Bob's mother) when the German bombers flattened the family home in Plaistow. The new house was virtually next door to an RAF fighter station. Bob Kimberley was captivated by the comings and goings at the station – he was particularly enthralled by the aerial dog fights and aerobatics. It came as no surprise to the family when he volunteered for the RAF and was accepted for aircrew training. He officially joined up on 31st May 1941.

After initial training at Babbacombe in Devon and Newquay in Cornwall, he was sent to Scotland to commence his early flying training. In January 1942 Bob had an early brush with death when he contracted pneumonia; he was lucky to pull through but went on to 'go solo' at the first attempt. He liked flying, it excited him and the demanding examination work proved a challenge to which he was equal. It was already clear that Bob Kimberley had the makings of a very fine pilot and, despite never coming to terms with service life, his dedication to the quest for his wings displayed a maturity which belied his years.

Bob Kimberley completed an intensive twelve-month training course in Canada (during which time he was awarded his wings) and he returned to England in the summer of 1943. Now a flight sergeant, he joined an Operational Training Unit and was finally attached to the Operational Squadron at RAF North Coates in Lincolnshire, flying Beaufighter fighter bombers with Coastal Command.

In November 1943 he became engaged to Chris, whom he had met prior to leaving for Canada. Chris was from Devon but was in Hornchurch for the duration of the war helping her aunt and uncle to run the local pub. They married in February 1944 and moved to a rented cottage near to the base in Lincolnshire.

On the evening of 10th September 1944 Bob Kimberley's squadron attacked enemy shipping off the Dutch coast. He did not return from the sortie. No news relevant to the circumstances of his death was ever forthcoming and it was eleven months before the Air Ministry confirmed that he had died in action.

Chris remarried in the late forties and now lives in Devon. Bob's beloved mother lived to a fine age and died in December 1987. Bob's younger brother Ken, lives in East Anglia with his wife Joan, Kim, the dog, and their cats Friday and Sam. Like his brother, Ken too has a fine artistic talent; this is shown to fine effect in his poignant illustrations which accompany his brother's letters.

Bob Kimberley might not have been the classic *Boy's Own* hero,

Bob and Chris on their wedding day – February 1944.

typically portrayed in films such as *The Dam Busters*, *Reach for the Sky* and *The Battle of Britain*. However, he was probably far more typical of the young men who formed the backbone of the RAF during the Second World War – confused, lonely and immature but no less brave or determined than their largely fictional counterparts. There is a certain amount of tragic irony in Bob Kimberley's letters which pinpoints, with great clarity, the futility of war. Here we have a young lad who sends his socks home to be washed and flies into a sulking fury if his mother does not write to him every day, and yet he blindly follows the path which will result in the ultimate sacrifice with great dedication and obvious pride. He is surely no less a hero for that.

A J Kimberley 1331518, aircraftman second class, summer 1941. (Second row, fifth from left.)

HISTORY OF RAF NORTH COATES

North Coates, Lincolnshire
113/TA375025. South of Grimsby between Northcoates Point and Horseshoe Point

This flat piece of land lies immediately behind the sand-dunes on the Lincolnshire coast and an aerodrome called North Coates Fitties was opened on this site in 1918. The resident unit was No 248 Squadron, 404 Flight, equipped with Short 225 aircraft, and this unit flew coastal patrols during the latter part of the First World War. In March 1919 it disbanded and in June the aerodrome was abandoned.

The Lincolnshire coast was perfect for armament training and in 1927 the Air Ministry bought eighty-eight acres of the First World War site with the intention of using it for annual summer armament practice camps for bomber squadrons, and the site was re-opened in that role. It continued in that capacity until 1934 when, during the Expansion period of the Royal Air Force, it was then decided to upgrade the site into a permanent airfield. The station opened in 1935 as No 2 Armament Training Camp and in January 1936 the Air Observers' School was formed. The following year these two units, equipped mainly with Wallace aircraft, merged to become 2 Air Armament School and in March 1938 this unit was renamed No 1 Air Observers' School. No 1 AOS, now flying Battles, remained here until the outbreak of war in September 1939 when it was then hastily moved to a quieter area in North Wales and the station was transferred to Coastal Command.

The station became RAF North Coates at the start of the Second World War, but during the first few months of the war had no resident flying units either because of fear of attack or because no squadrons were available and housed only ground units. These included No 2 Recruit Training Pool and No 1 Ground Defence School, the forerunner of the RAF regiment, whose role was to train airmen for airfield defence. Then, in late February 1940, the first squadron arrived flying Blenheim IVfs and a few Battles. This was No 235 Squadron which was followed in March by two more squadrons, Nos 236 and 248. Both of these were equipped with fighter versions of the Blenheim and these long-range fighter squadrons of Coastal Command patrolled far out over the North Sea.

The airfield had by now been extended and the single runway was 1,400 yards long. This pointed towards North Coates village and the sea, ending almost on the beach. A piece of perimeter track was laid to link each end of the runway to the buildings that were all grouped at the northern end of this very isolated outpost.

When the Germans invaded Denmark and Norway in April 1940, Nos 235, 236 and 248 Squadrons moved south to join Fighter Command. That same month No 22 Squadron arrived equipped with the new Bristol Beaufort. This unit was accompanied in May by No 812 Squadron, Fleet Air Arm, whose Fairey Swordfish looked very out of place alongside the Beauforts. However, these aircraft did their task well. Together with No 22 Squadron they attacked enemy shipping and it was this role that the station assumed for the remainder of the war. During April No 22 Squadron sent a detachment to St Eval, Cornwall, and from there they

Flying a sortie off the Dutch coast, 1944.

attacked the German battlecruiser *Gneisenau* in Brest harbour. For his part in this operation Flying Officer Keith Campbell was awarded a posthumous Victoria Cross.

Over the next three years many units operated from North Coates. In April 1941, No 42 Squadron arrived, equipped with Beauforts. One of their members was Pilot Officer Philpott, DFC, who later became one of the escapees in the now famous 'wooden horse' breakout, for which he was awarded the Military Cross. The following month, No 816 Squadron, FAA, took over its sister unit, No 812 Squadron's commitment. June saw the departure of Nos 22 and 42 Squadrons together with the Swordfishes of No 816, and the arrival of No 86 equipped with Beauforts.

On 9th July Lincolnshire saw the arrival of another Canadian squadron when the Lockheed Hudsons of No 407 (Canadian) Squadron moved into North Coates. This unit was engaged on anti-shipping strikes which were carried out almost at sea level, making the operation highly dangerous. However, the Canadians, with the help of their Commanding Officer, Wing Commander Styles, soon became experts in their task and were most successful during their period at North Coates, damaging 150,000 tons of Axis shipping.

During October the pace slowed down when two non-operational units arrived at the airfield, these being No 6 Anti-Aircraft Co-Operation Unit flying Lysanders and an Air-Sea Rescue unit, No 278 Squadron, equipped with Lysanders and Ansons. A Walrus amphibian was later added for pick-up work. The role of these units was air-sea rescue along the Lincolnshire and Yorkshire coasts and involved dinghy drops and spotting missions. The ASR unit worked in conjunction with

22 Motor Launch Unit based at nearby Grimsby. With the arrival of these units the station was again congested and many of the aircraft had to use the airfield at Donna Nook a few miles down the coast.

Through the winter months the station continued operations then, in February 1942, Nos 86 and 407 Squadrons departed to be replaced by Nos 53 and 59 Squadrons. Both units were equipped with Hudsons and a high proportion of the pilots were Australian. On the 24th of the month Flight Lieutenant R C Guthrie attacked a convoy which consisted of seven merchant ships and four naval escorts. His Hudson attacked the largest ship with his four 250 lb bombs but in the process he was repeatedly hit and under great difficulty managed to crash-land at Bircham Newton.

No 217 Squadron equipped with Beauforts, also arrived in February and this unit stayed a short time before moving to Ceylon. February also saw the arrival of a second-line FAA unit, No 776 Squadron, equipped with the standard Blackburn Roc fighters. Also, 6 AACU was replaced by a detachment from 7 AACU.

By the end of March 1942, No 59 Squadron had become operational and was sharing operational duties with 53 Squadron, but in May both units were replaced by the Hudsons of Nos 206 and 224 Squadrons which remained for the summer months. On 5th June No 415 (RCAF) Squadron arrived equipped with Hampdens which were being used as torpedo bombers. This was the only Canadian Torpedo Bomber squadron formed overseas and on 30th July 1942 it moved to Wick in Scotland.

Coastal Command continued attacking enemy shipping but the German ships were well armed with anti-

Bob Kimberley in command of his 'Beau'.

aircraft guns and even though the anti-shipping strike units had proved fairly successful, other and more effective means had to be discovered. North Coates was selected to try out some new tactics and, in August 1942, No 143 Squadron arrived, equipped with Beaufighters. The following month Air Ministry agreed to nominate this aircraft as the standard strike machine for Coastal Command. September saw the arrival of two further Beaufighter squadrons, Nos 236 and 254. Of all the many units operated from North Coates, the station was to become best known for these squadrons, which formed the 'North Coates Wing'.

This was a strike wing based on the pattern which had proved successful at Malta, in which a squadron of fast torpedo bombers was accompanied by one or more squadrons of equal performance that could concentrate on suppressing enemy anti-aircraft fire with their cannon fire and bombs. No 254 Squadron was to be the Beaufighter torpedo squadron while Nos 143 and 236 were the two Beaufighter 'anti-flak' squadrons.

By the end of the year the Wing had made its first sortie but it miscarried badly and the squadrons were immediately withdrawn for intensive training until April 1943 when they once again became operational. During June the rocket-armed Beaufighter became available and the Wing was a huge success. This led to the formation of a second Wing at Leuchars. In August No 143 Squadron departed but the Wing continued to operate with the remaining two squadrons and it was so successful that the enemy had to curtail trade from Rotterdam and route the iron ore and associated cargoes through Emden.

In February 1944, No 143 Squadron returned but in May it moved to Manston, Kent, to take part in operation 'Overlord'. The status of North Coates on 6th June was No 236 and 254 Squadrons, both equipped with Beaufighter X aircraft and in No 16 Group. The North Coates Wing continued to inflict crushing blows on the enemy shipping with their under wing rocket projectiles and in September was rejoined by No 143 Squadron. Its stay was brief, however, for in October it moved to Banff in Scotland to help form a new Strike Wing.

The North Coates Wing continued with its successful tactics and, in 1945, No 254 Squadron began to partly re-equip with the Mosquito Mark XVIII which had been produced specifically for Coastal Command carrying a 57 mm (6 pr) Molins gun. However, very few saw any operational service for only twenty-seven were produced.

During the first week in May 1945, Nos 236 and 254 Squadrons were credited with five U-boats sunk but their war days were nearly over and towards the end of the month the Wing disbanded. That same month No 236 Squadron moved out, followed in June by 254 Squadron. During operations from North Coates ninety-seven decorations had been won and 484 airmen had lost their lives.

RAF Museum, Hendon

11

BABBACOMBE, DEVON

Saturday 31st May 1941

Dear Mum & all,

Arrived safe but worn out at 4 o'clock. Have got majority of ordinary RAF kit already. Pretty good fit I think mum. Got decent bed in decent hotel. Decent sergeant and decent blokes. Decent so far. I think food will be OK. Will be here one week then moved to initial training wing (ground drill, maths exams, etc.). About six weeks there and then I don't know what comes next. Anyway, things will be OK. If I don't pass all this training and tests, I can do something else. Hope you will be OK. Hope you felt alright after train scramble.

Best love

Bob X X X

BABBACOMBE, DEVON

Sunday 1st June 1941

I hope that you write
pretty soon. Have
chummed up with two decent
blokes already. It makes
a lot of difference.
Girls are out of question
at moment.

Dear Mum & all

Things a bit better today. Tomorrow inoculation (they inject you in the nipples of all places) and vaccination and blood grouping. Sounds bad but I don't think there's much need to worry. They do all three in about thirty seconds. After-affects are generally a slight fever and swelling, but you go on light duties for two days. I feel pretty fit. Everybody is nervy. Food pretty good. I hope you are feeling OK. We've done very little today nothing at all this afternoon. Up at about 6.00 am. Bed at 9.30 pm. Wore kit this morning (boots!).

PS We'll have to have a holiday in this place one day Mum.

Have got majority of ordinary RAF kit already.

NEWQUAY, CORNWALL

23rd July 1941

Dear Mum & all,

....I'm glad you are all keeping well. I feel fit. Food here is jolly good. Plenty of it. Plenty of butter, etc. I feel better settled now, I know now what the general outline for the next two months will be. I have never worked so hard before – have been out only two evenings last week for half an hour each evening, and that was only to supper at the NAAFI.

First exam is this Wednesday – it is maths (my worst subject). If you fail you cease training as a pilot. I don't know what sort of job you get then. If I fail I should try to get into a drawing job. They need plenty of drawings of planes all the time. If you pass, you have to pass in navigation, and morse, before you go to flying school. There are other subjects, and if you pass these they help. But, maths, navigation and morse code are the most important. Prospects of leave are good for those who pass, but if you fail there is still a chance.

Today is Sunday and we get most of the day off (after church parade and inspection). It gives you breathing space. I'm on guard tonight. Newquay has lovely sands, we have PT on the beach. Plaistow Secondary is evacuated down here (I haven't had a chance to find them yet), and two or three other West Ham schools.

I'm sending two pairs of the socks you made home to be washed, and one pair of RAF socks. Socks and pyjamas are the only things I would like you to wash. The RAF laundry does the other things OK. I'm also sending one very dirty handkerchief – I used it to put 'silvo' polish on my buttons. I'm sorry but I had no dusters at first. Thanks ever so much for that parcel. Take care of yourselves.

All my love

Bob X X X X X

PS Your allowance will be 7/- per week mum while I'm here. They stopped the first 7/- yesterday, Friday 21st of July. I expect you'll have to wait for the book, but you'll get back pay OK. I asked about

Polishing the lino in the CO's room.

it. I would appreciate another 5/- book of stamps. Thanks for your stamped envelopes mum. Thanks for offering to let me have some money if I ever wanted it. If you could send me 5/- stamps and 5/- money next week I will be OK – I'm not short at present, you can't get out to spend much really. When you send me parcels, please send a bit of brown paper for me to send you parcels back. You can't get it here. Those carriers are a good idea for parcels.

NEWQUAY, CORNWALL

Thursday

Dear Mum & all

I expect you'll be a bit surprised to hear from me again so soon – well I don't want you to get worried, but there's a possibility of the majority of my flight going abroad for our flying training. Now, don't get worried about it, there's a chance that we won't have to go. What I wanted to avoid was having to let you know at the last moment – and that would have been a very big shock – so I thought it was best to keep you worried for a bit, better than let it be a big shock.

Now, if I do have to go abroad it will be to Canada – that's pretty certain (but although that's not much information, I shouldn't say much about it). We will at any rate most likely stop at Newquay till end of next week, take our exams and then either have a week's leave and stop in England for flying, or go abroad after either three or four days' leave, or, what is more than likely, go abroad after a forty-eight-hour pass. Now, I'm sorry to say the last case seems probable at the moment, for three quarters of our fifty chaps, including me, were interviewed by the Wing Commander today, and although he was very vague over everything, it is definitely in the air that we are likely to be going abroad for our flying. Now if I do only get forty-eight hours leave, you can see I should only have a few hours with you, and I expect you would be as pleased about that as I would, so would you be prepared Mum and Ken and perhaps Pop too, to come down here to Newquay, so that we could have forty-eight hours together.

I expect what you've just read has bowled you over – it's rather knocked the wind out of my sails and all my pals. All sorts of wild rumours are knocking about – in fact it's not even authorative yet about anybody at all going abroad, let alone me in particular. But I thought it would be best for you to know in case. Now what ever you do Mum, please don't get ever so worried for it is just as likely that we won't have to go. If you remember Ron Leggo was surprised to go and didn't. But the point is, today we've done practically nil bar this interview and the sergeant says we've as good as had our leave.

You can guess how I feel – a week off the exams and getting home and they drop this new bombshell. I don't feel much like working now. I wouldn't mind so much if leave – six days or even three or four days was certain – I wouldn't care so much, but there you are, it's no good, you first have to take it with as good a heart as possible. There's rumours too that our exams will be put forward. I'm on guard tonight too – what a happy world.

They say you have a good time in Canada – and stand a better chance of getting through for certain. Your training is better. If I did go and got through OK I should come back a sergeant pilot, and one with real good training. I'm afraid it might mean four – six months, but after that I'd have a whole month with you at home.

We wouldn't be able to get letters to each other so often – that's the worst part of it, but think, I could be sent to Scotland or Northern England for flying training and I'd just as likely not see you for ages. Some of the chaps who were on ground jobs haven't had leave for nine months. We'd hear from each other at least once a fortnight but, as I've said before, there's a chance this worry is all for nothing – it's far from certain, so don't worry too much Mum.

I shall let you know as soon as I possibly can for certain what's going to happen, and how much leave, if any, I'll get – then it'll be up to you if I get only forty-eight hours. If you want me to come home and be with you for a few hours, or if you'd sooner come down here.

You can't realise how rotten I feel about having to worry you like this – but I thought it was for the better and I'll write again tomorrow. If I do have to go, you must look at it like this – I'll be perfectly safe, safer than in England, and I'm not going abroad to fight like the poor devils had to in France and now out East. My training would take longer abroad and it would probably be at least eight months before I got going and of course I might fail the exams. You could say, fail then, but what's the good, I can't be like that.

Well Mum and Ken and Pop, don't let this letter upset you if you can help it, as I've said, it might never happen, but I thought it best to tell you. I'm not ever so miserable for I know the RAF a bit now – they love to keep you on a bit of toast for nothing, so again don't get worried. I shall write tomorrow even if I know nothing definite. Goodbye for now, and look after yourselves.

All my love Bob

PS Thank you for your letter and 10/- mum, I've got 30/- by me now, and pay day is tomorrow!

NEWQUAY, CORNWALL

Friday

Dear Mum & all,

....Had a bit of luck tonight. Majority of the fellows had to go to RAF cinema from 7.00 – 9.30 pm, it was what they call an 'in-line piquet'. (That's a sort of easy guard duty.) Well, my two pals and me were given the job of polishing the lino in the CO's room. We soon got that done as you can guess, then climbed out of the back of the hotel, down the fire escape, thus getting past sergeant OK and had a good tuck in at the NAAFI while the rest were at cinema. Then got back OK and I've had two lovely hours to myself in our room (three of us live in it), and have used it to get all my little things, and odds and ends, in perfect order. Don't think Mum, that you don't have time to look after yourself (I shave every day now, bath twice a week and have not missed washing my hair one week yet – blinking marvellous I reckon), but extra classes don't leave you much time at night, and all the time you have that 'pushed-on' feeling, that gives a big strain on your nerves. At times we all get very ratty, and snap each others blinking heads off over the merest trifles. I think this course is really disgusting – it worries most of us stiff – but as Ron Leggo wrote, if you get through here OK there isn't so much brain work at flying school, and far less red tape. Well, everyday brings me nearer to leave. I expect you realise what it means to us and it'll be a bitter disappointment if I don't get it. After telling us that we must pass everything to get this leave, we found out the other day that exam results aren't known till you're on your way. That is every one but the morse exam, which you take a week before the others. I am

We climbed out of the back of the hotel, down the fire escape, thus getting past the sergeant.

pretty good at this, the only thing that worries me is getting panicky and not being able to think quick enough when the crucial moment comes.

The exam consists of receiving seventy words and figures. The letters are sent at a rate of six a minute (you've probably heard some on wireless accidentally at times). That is 'sound' morse. You are allowed five mistakes in seventy to pass. You also have to send seventy letters at the same speed to your testing officer. Then there is 'light' morse, from a camp (another seventy words) and you also have to send this – it's a flickering light really about a quarter of a mile away on top of a building. Your whole testing takes only about a quarter of an hour, I could do it now under ordinary conditions, but it's different in an exam. Still, we'll see, if I do fail, (sometimes they are lenient and push you through, if you've been trying), I'll be just unlucky, thats all, and shall have to wait (some of the fellows are army chaps – sergeants and corporals and haven't had leave since xmas). Oh well, Mum, Sunday is near and that means an easy day. Last Sunday I went to a little place, out about a mile, and had a lovely tea for a 1/- at a farm with Eric, my pal. The roses round here are lovely – I wonder what our place looks like, and Hornchurch. I'll have to stop here, it's late. Heard from Aunt Gert this week. Tell her not to be offended if I don't write immediately – I haven't got time to write very well, to anyone but you. But I shall write to Aunt Liz this weekend. Hope you're still enjoying your job. Tell Ken he doesn't know how well off he is, 3/- rise, and tell him never to get fed up with home, at the moment I'd honestly sooner be at home than in heaven – if there's such a place. Home means heaven, I reckon, to all the poor buggers in the RAF. Cheerio, Mum & all. I'm not fed up or miserable. If I don't get leave in two weeks don't you be disappointed too much – thank God there's letter writing, and I must get a leave eventually – of course there's always the possibility of the war ending one of these fine days. I don't get very homesick, 'cause there's no time to think about it. The work is hard but some of it's very interesting. You're absorbing new and useful knowledge all the time. I've learnt more in the last two months than I've learnt since I left school. Well, I'll really have to stop now – I'm hoping to hear from you again very soon. I could go on writing – but it's part lights out and there's rifle drill first thing tomorrow. You go from one extreme to the other on this course: one minute your sweating, marching and

… and had a good tuck in at the NAAFI.

drilling, the next minute listening to lectures and plotting courses on charts.

Cheerio everybody, look after yourselves for me.

Love Bob

PS Have also heard from Joan Leggo.

PSS Very IMPORTANT. Do you think you could send me 5/- to 10/- every week Mum. That just does me OK, and I can still keep £1 at back of me just in case I ever want it.

Had a lovely tea for a shilling.

Saturday evening

Dear Mum & all

There isn't anything more definite to tell you. All I know is that a certain number of blokes have got to be chosen from our lot at Newquay, and if I pass my exams OK during next week I will probably go. Now if I am chosen there is a good chance of three – four days leave from 25th till the 29th from here. On the other hand they may hold us here till the 29th and send us to the embarkation port. If the convoy is ready you get no leave, but generally you get it. So I may get one leave from here, and then go abroad; or leave from embarkation port or two leaves – one from here and one from embarkation port. I am pretty confident then that we'll get leave of some sort. Now, please don't worry if I am chosen, and don't be terribly upset if I got no leave at all – it'll only be for a few months more. But, as I've said, I shall get some. Of course if I fail the exams I shan't go, and there's a good chance of that too, though I don't want it to happen, now I've got this far. I hope my letters haven't made you feel too bad Mum, I almost wished I'd left it to chance, and not told you till I came home on leave. Could you possibly send me a couple of pounds next week (send a PO for £2 if I were you – if you send it just in a letter it is not too safe, and if you make it a registered one then I'll have a lot of trouble to get it from headquarters here).

...Well cheerio Mum and all, I'm not miserable so don't you be (the war will be over soon). It's tea-time now so I'll close. Shall write if anything definite is told us. If not, shall write again so as you get the letter by about Thursday. Please send that money, won't you? I might have enough already, but you never know.

Love Bob X X X X X

There's rifle drill first thing tomorrow.

Sunday

Dear Mum & all,

Hope you are all well. I received your parcel OK. It was jolly good – especially blue bags and Silvikrin (thanks Ken). I shan't say much in this letter Mum, nothing else of any importance has happened – we are just plodding on now towards final exams. The only thing to spoil today is I've got to go to the dentists at 11.30 am (I've only got to have a little bit of tooth taken out that the Hornchurch dentist left in). Not much that. Went to pictures last night, first night out for three weeks. Going out this afternoon to have a relaxed bit of swotting, sun-bathing and tuck-in at the cafe. That reminds me, Mum, sorry to have to ask you, but I could do with some more money soon, if you could manage it. Most of my money goes on cakes and tea breaks during the day and suppers at night. (RAF don't supply anything from 6.00 pm (tea-time) to breakfast). I have also had to buy books, toothpaste, etc.

Have just come back from the dentists (had that bit out and I stopped). It's put me off dinner but it's OK. If you send me any other parcels, could you send me some cakes if you can. (My two pals get cakes and things – they always give me some, and I feel mean about not returning it). Hope it's not a cheek asking Mum, but you don't realise how we look forward to anything like that.

Well, Mum, there's nothing else to say just yet. It's a beautiful day here – I'm more than pleased to have joined up during this weather, it makes a tremendous difference. I'd love to be home today and be going out for a ride – there's nothing I'd like better. Honestly it would be a pleasure to have a bus ride at the moment. Have not heard from Ken yet. Well, cheerio everybody. If I pass the rest of my exams I should be home on 26th or 27th of this month. Look after yourselves.

Love Bob

PS We are the second oldest flight here now, and consider ourselves quite old sweats. The oldest flight is due to leave in a fortnight. That'll be the day when we get packed up to come home. I want to get home, naturally, more than anything in the world at the moment, except the end of the war. That's what I'm afraid of – getting nervy in my morse exam when we all know that leave is decided by it. Oh well, if I don't get it, I don't, but I'll do my absolute best.

NEWQUAY, CORNWALL

Dear Ken,

Thanks for your letter, I received it yesterday. Don't be offended if this letter of mine is neither long nor interesting, but the CO has discovered that I used to be a commercial artist, and he has given me umpteen odd jobs to do and I want to get this letter posted this morning before I start. The tobacco is for Pop, if it's any good to him.

…You say Bill came round, with apples too. Apples – I haven't seen one for months. I'm having a very easy time here, but I shall be glad to be moving again. Very glad! Glad to here that you've met that fellow you mentioned, Ken, and that you may join that club. Do you do much biking now? It seems ages since the days when we went cycling at weekends. It'll be grand when those days return.

But I can't grumble for I shall be posted near home eventually – either Regent's Park or Cambridge. Probably both. It doesn't matter, for I shall be able to get home weekends from either place. Well, I'll say cheerio for a bit Ken, and please write again.

Bob

The CO has discovered I used to be a commercial artist.

It seems ages since the days when we went cycling at weekends.

Thursday 14th August 1941

Dear Mum & all,

Thanks very much for the 10/- I received yesterday. Believe me, I should have had to go without cups of tea during the day, suppers, etc until Friday if I hadn't received it, for my pals are in a stony state too. I was thankful mum.

Well it looks as if I shall be here a little longer. I told you I was waiting for the Cambridge posting to come through, didn't I? Half my old flight, and half my special pals, are posted to Hatfield this Friday. Hatfield, mind you – probably easier to get home at weekends than Cambridge. Oh well, I'm having a terribly easy time at Newquay, now not much work and all evenings free, bar about one in ten days. They don't know what to do with us.

What makes you think Mum that Joyce is sweet on me? You remember Dorothy, well, she writes to me pretty often. I haven't written to Bill or Alf yet. I will do so soon. Before I forget Mum, is there another pair of my pants at home – I mean those without loops. I'm wearing RAF underclothes this week but I'm not struck on them, so could you send me another pair if possible. The RAF vests are not too bad. They're blessed awful looking things but who cares? I wonder too, if I left a RAF shirt at home, on my leave. I should have three, but I can only lay hands on two of them at the moment. Don't worry about it, it doesn't matter a lot, but if there's another kit inspection, I may have to account for it. We get paid this Friday, but won't get LAC money – it'll be a few weeks before that comes through. Glad to hear you're having a week off with Pop – I shouldn't worry too much about that job. Glad, too, to hear that Ken is going to write. Well, I think that's all I've got to say at present, Mum. I'm living in hopes of getting posted now, for the quicker I get to Cambridge the quicker I'll get home again, I hope, but in the meantime things could be a million times worse for me. It's a bit boring doing practically nothing all day, but it's better than sweating your guts out. So cheerio for now Mum, look after yourselves, and here's hoping to see you soon. Already I feel as if I hadn't seen you for months instead of what is it? A fortnight.

All my love

Bob X X X X X X

We most likely will be posted to Regent's Park for our eye training.

NEWQUAY, CORNWALL

Dear Mum & all,

I thought I'd write to you again before receiving an answer to my last letter. It seems now that we most likely will be posted to Regent's Park for our eye training. What do you think of that? It will mean that I'll get home every weekend (though I probably shan't be there long), and from what I've gathered from fellows who've been there you can get a sleeping out pass nearly every night.

…Well Mum, it looks as if I may see you much sooner than I expected. Don't let's bank on it though. I'll write again about Wednesday or Thursday, and perhaps I'll have something more definite to tell you then. Don't send those things I asked for now. It doesn't matter if you've posted them already, though. Could you send me another 10/- next week too, just in case I need it. You see, although we are now LAC's we're not getting LAC money yet. It's a racket. Well, I'll close now. Here's hoping to see you soon.

All my love

Bob X X X X X X X

PERTHSHIRE, SCOTLAND

Early January 1942

Dear Mum & all,

I expect you're wondering what's happened since Monday. I haven't been able to write before. The train journey didn't help me get rid of that cold, but after keeping us messing about a few hours when we got here (they even took our photo's and did we look wrecks!) I managed to report sick. They put me to bed, and already I feel much better. There's nothing much wrong I know, a couple of days in bed the MO said and I'll be OK…

The train journey didn't help me to get rid of my cold!

They put me to bed and I feel better already.

PERTHSHIRE, SCOTLAND

Friday 16th January 1942

Dear Mum,

I'm ever so sorry that I've not been able to write before. You see, I was a week in Station Sick Quarters, and then they decided to send me to hospital. It's nothing to worry about mum, honestly – bronchitis. The reason they sent me here was that I developed very high temperatures and they thought hospital was the best place. They've put me on a liquid diet for a couple of days, I felt groggy last night, but feel fine this morning. I shall be OK now and be home on sick leave in a week or two I expect. It seems as though I've had a run of bad luck, but the good is coming along now I should think. This is the first time I've laid in bed a whole week, and I can't say that I like it. And I thought that bronchitis was nothing...

PERTHSHIRE, SCOTLAND

Tuesday 27th January 1942

Dear Mum,

Thanks for your very very welcome letter received this morning. Feel better myself though terribly weak. Chest clearer doctor said on his inspection of our ward. I must be patient I suppose and please ask Chris to wait a little longer for an answer to her letter. I have a little pleurisy in the bottom left hand side I heard the doctor say, but antibiotics will probably get rid of that. My biggest fight is not to worry over things. This affair has certainly shown me a thing or two. It has made up for the good time I had prior to leaving London. Very cold here. Snow, no transport, very hard on everybody...

Saturday 31st January 1942

Dear Mum,

I feel better still today so far (morning). Now that I am getting better I suppose they've decided to tell me a bit more. The night sister told me last night that I've had bronchial pneumonia, and have been a bit delirious – I hope sincerely that my earlier letter didn't put the wind up you. Doctor yesterday said I was getting better slowly but surely. Anyway I feel more normal and better in myself now. I'm sure of that. I'm on a light diet, and get malt occasionally now, and that proves I'm in the recuperating stage. Sleep is still difficult but that is still to be expected.

…Well Mum, it's grand to know I'm improving, and one of these very near days I'll be on my feet again, and things should be a lot different.

I'll close here for now.

All my love
your loving

Bob X X X X X

PS Have not heard from you yesterday and expect our letters will cross but don't worry for time being. I'll wait for next one before writing again. But I've known you wanted as many letters as possible from me.

PERTHSHIRE, SCOTLAND

Wednesday 4th February 1942

Dear Mum,

I have just received your letter (11 am WED) written on Monday and it cheered me up as all letters from home do. I am still improving OK,

The sister told me that I've had bronchial pneumonia.

but the doctor says it will take time naturally. My chest is practically cleared up and as soon as the little pleurisy left over from the illness (don't worry this happens always) has been cleared up by poultices (ought to be couple of days), I shall be allowed up more and more each day. I slept well (eight hours) last night but had only two hours on Saturday. It isn't my chest that stops sleep now – I'm not considered really ill at all now of course and I don't feel ill: nothing like I did – it's just bed soreness, and if you start twisting and turning of course you make it worse. Anyway I'm not put out too much by that sort of thing now – it's just left over feelings and lack of exercise. And of course I'm still pleased as punch to know that the worst of the real trouble is far behind and I've learnt a little to control impatience.

…About Chris – I wrote to her days ago (Saturday morning a fellow took it with him to the post. I expect she's got it now and will be answering it. I'll be writing again if I don't get an answer).

Well Mum, thanks for everything, I don't suppose I'll ever be able to repay half of what you've done for me, but one of these days maybe; in fact it's sure that we'll be happy thoroughly again.

I'll close here for now. Look after yourselves.

All my love

Bob X X X X X

Perthshire, Scotland

Thursday 5th February 1942

Dear Mum & all,

I am pleased to say I'm feeling stronger and hungrier each day even though I get plenty of good food. That's a good sign I can hear you saying.

Doctor examined me this morning and said I've still got a bit of 'friction', he calls it, in the bottom left hand side of my lungs. But that is much better I know myself. I have slept well the last couple of nights and eating well in the day will help me recover quickly now. It is five weeks today since I arrived in Scotland and went to bed, and

I'm taking a bit longer than is usual in the case to get up, but the reason is that my illness developed very slowly thus using up more resistance than the usual cases of pneumonia. Therefore I suppose I must be patient still, and expect myself to take a bit longer before being allowed up for the first time. I've got no pain at all in my chest and back now so it can't be long.

Well Mum, how is everybody at home still. I hope things are going smoothly for everyone.

...Oh, I say: I've just received your parcel. It was lovely. Everything I wanted most of all at the moment. You've done marvels for me. I'll ask if I can have one of those tins of fruit with tea tonight and I can share it with my pal the schoolmaster fellow who is just recovering like me from pneumonia. I haven't even finished your cake yet and I've got enough stuff in my locker for a siege now. Thanks ever so much Mum and thank Chris for me will you and I expect good old Ken did the parcel up. I owe you all such a lot. I gave the cigarettes away – I hope you don't mind. I don't want to chance any just yet, and the fellow I gave 'em to has done a lot for me since I've been here. The biscuits are a special treat too.

I have not heard from Chris yet?

Well Mum, these letters from home and parcels do buck you up no end and you know how grateful I am. I've got two pairs of silk stockings in my case which have been waiting five weeks to be sent to you. As soon as I'm allowed out to the post office in the village I'll send 'em. Of course they won't make up for the stuff you send me, nowhere near, but I can't hope to repay you.

One of these days I shall I hope in some way or other...

PERTHSHIRE, SCOTLAND

10th February 1942

...Well Mum, I hope this letter doesn't seem too selfish but God if you don't look after yourself first no one else will (except your own people). I hope you understand me.

Have not heard from Chris! If you see her (it doesn't worry me too much if you don't) you can say I shan't write until I get answer from the last letter of mine.

I'm not upset – that sort of thing leaves me fairly unmoved at the moment. I'm not even very bitter. I just don't care much at the moment. As long as I hear from you and keep getting better as quickly as possible everything else can wait, I really honesty mean this. Ask Ken if it's true when I say that...

PERTHSHIRE, SCOTLAND

Wednesday 11th February 1942

Dear Mum, Ken & Pop

Well Mum, thanks for your letter I received today. Don't think I'm grumbling too much but that letter you got Friday was written on Wednesday, I received yours this morning. That's a week isn't it for an answer to reach one another.

Please, if you can, answer my letters the same day, and I will do the same. You can't possibly realise no matter how you try, how letters are looked forward to from home.

So let's try and get a letter to each other every day. Please Mum. I've given up all ideas of any letter from Chris – I just don't care now about her.

You needn't write a long letter – as short as you like but just let me hear more often.

...And could you send me a parcel of grub, like the other, once a week. I know it must take a lot of time and trouble to get the stuff together, but if you only knew how it helps.

Of course don't get the idea that I'm starved, far from it, but fruit helps your bowels and believe me after a month like mine, even with medicine, it takes a bit of effort. And all those other things you sent are each one a special treat. Of course you can't wolf the lot yourself because other fellows give you some of theirs...

Tuesday 3rd March 1942

Dear Mum, Ken & Pop

Once more I have some very good news for you. I am being sent convalescent today. I am so sorry I couldn't let you know before this but I wasn't told till last night myself. I don't know where I am going (one of the fellows is going with me – a very nice quiet chap) but I will let you know my new address as soon as absolutely possible.

I expect you have sent me another parcel. I have received all the others on Tuesday afternoons, so if you have I will receive this one today also I expect. I haven't finished all the other stuff – the cake, and of course I have lots of that lovely strawberry jam left. If I leave here before it arrives don't worry it'll reach me OK.

The sister is giving me a pass to Scone so that I can see them and get some odds and ends.

I have been out in the bitter cold quite often now, though well wrapped up, and shall be OK now I'm sure.

A bus will take me most of way to the 'drome today, and tomorrow an ambulance will take us right to the door of the convalescent home…

Leslie House
Fife, Scotland

Friday 6th March 1942

Dear Mum, Ken & Pop

Well everybody, I'm feeling fine still. Leslie House is OK but the weather is lousy again. If we have any more snow we'll be well and truly snowed in. It is cold too, and because of deep snow my pal and I didn't think it worth getting an afternoon pass or worth going to the pictures last night. Instead we stayed in and played table-tennis most of the time (I feel a bit stiff this morning) and read. It snowed heavy last night and I expect we'll stay in again today. The snow had nearly all gone on Tuesday too.

The food is good, hot and very well cooked by the housekeeper. Though of course a parcel will make life much brighter, too.

The bloke whose house it is, a sir someone or other, his wife and her secretary-companion, a French countess, came into the lounge last night and watched us playing cards. The old fellow is a very nice old gentleman (he wore evening dress with a red velvet dinner jacket) and was very friendly. The two women were also. The French countess was a blessed dream. Very beautiful and marvellously dressed in a black evening gown and just a fur, all of them were very pleasant and unaffected. Of course they talked very Oxfordian, but it was natural to them. The fellows say the countess has a marvellous voice and I've heard her playing some overture or other in another part of the house. The fellows are invited by them to whist drives and dances.

The grounds are a terrific size – as big as Wansted Park I should imagine. They would be ideal in summer but of course you can't go strolling around in drifts of snow.

The village is at the gates, but the drive is easily half a mile long. I'm itching to go out, for although the place is fine, time lags. There are plenty of nurses and not many fellows so we have to do very little but laze about.

We haven't had any eggs for breakfast, but we get a morning cup of tea in bed and don't have to get up till 7.30 a.m. We get a cup of hot milk, or ovaltine at night, with a couple of cakes. Breakfast at 8.00 am. Dinner at 12.00. Tea at 5.00 pm. Bed at 9.00 pm. Lights out at 10.00 pm, except on picture nights (Tuesday, Thursday & Friday). Seats are reserved for you.

I shall be here for two or three weeks, then back to the hospital for a final exam.

The doctor is a civvy doctor. He came yesterday and examined my chest thoroughly. He said I was doing very well. I don't have malt now, but when I get out to the village I shall buy a jar for myself. It won't do any harm and I am very well off for money.

The place on the whole is very easy going (nothing like the red-tape and inspection of Bridge of Earn [the General Hospital]). It is OK and although I'm bored at times I am content. I am getting tons of rest – much more than at the hospital, and the whole place is a much happier affair.

I shan't be able to phone today I expect, so I will phone you on Wednesday if the snow will allow it.

Well cheerio for now, Mum, and look after yourselves.

Your loving son,
as ever,

Bob X X X X X X X X

An ambulance will take us right to the door of the convalescent home.

10th March 1942

Dear Mum & all

With the start of a new week the weather looks more promising. There's a lovely sky this morning and the sun is already melting the drifts. My chest is fine now. I've had a bit of a sore throat for a couple of days but it is much better today. But doctor won't let me go out till at least Wednesday. I like this place very much. Nurses are very kind, everything bar sugar and butter ration is really first rate. I am enjoying myself OK though of course everything is very quiet and I'm itching to get outside in the fresh air. But weather is very treacherous here, and I'm fairly content to do as I'm told. By the time I get home you'll never know I've had an illness. I don't get any pains or trouble at all from my chest now. Get rid of this bit of cold and I'll be OK. It's not a cold really – just catarrh. I don't have any medicine or malt now, but when I get out to the village (or my pal can get in today) I'll get some. I don't suppose the doctor thinks I need any now. He's very good by the way. But it won't do any harm, and I've got nothing else much to spend my money on.

This place is very homely – the butler cleans all the boots when the fellows have been out, and everything runs smoothly and you have to do practically nothing. So far I've washed up once, and swept and tidied the lounge…

Tuesday 31st March 1942

Dear Mum, Ken & Pop

I have been a bit neglectful the last few days as regarding writing, but I've had so little news to tell you.

I am still feeling fine, and I hope everyone at home is keeping well.

The bloke whose house it is, a sir someone or other, his wife and her secretary-companion, a French countess, came into the lounge last night and watched us playing cards.

I am going back to the Bridge of Earn this Friday, another step nearer home – it won't be long now.

I have had a very nice time here, but I am getting a bit bored with the place and want to do something soon. I do hope that I get my sick leave but if I'm unlucky I shall at least get seven days ordinary leave very soon.

The weather has been dull and wet these last few days and that makes the place much less appealing. I am itching to get home and I hope they get my final exam over quickly at the Bridge.

I am longing too, to get into a decent suit again – I'm not in love with hospital blues. It'll be good to feel that tweed suit on my back again. It's funny how you look forward to little things like that. And a green tie and shirt, oh boy!

My hair has been falling out in handfuls since my illness, and that hasn't pleased me, but I expect it'll grow a bit thicker as time goes on. It got so long it curled over my shirt collar. Anyway, you can do without your hair.

I had a game of clock golf yesterday in the grounds. Boy! You should have seen the holes I dug in the turf. We had another table tennis match last night.

There are quite a few of us going back on Friday. I'm looking forward to it – I feel fit for absolutely anything now.

The parcel is going well, Mum. I shall take the sugar and butter back to the hospital with me. (By the way, I did write to thank you for it, didn't I Mum? I'd almost forgotten.)

...I haven't heard from Chris for over a week. She's a rum girl, but I'm as bad. I write very seldom to her. I'm not interested just now.

Has Ken started taking any girls around. I was surprised to hear he fancies the navy, though I fancied that too at first. Still there's plenty of time for him yet. I suppose I should write to Aunt Liz soon. Have you heard from John yet? He owes me a letter.

Well Mum, this is all for just now. I'll soon be home. Look after yourself. I hope Pop's alright now.

Your loving son
as always

Bob X X X X X X

This place is very homely – the butler cleans all the boots when the fellows have been out.

April, 1942

…One thing more than anything, I'm looking forward to when I get home are nice long walks on sunny days and coming back glowing and feeling fine.

Oh boy! I am looking forward to that leave and seeing you all again. It seems ages now since I used to bunk home from Regent's Park.

Oh well! A month or more is not long when you're feeling pretty fit, and able to get out, so I don't mind.

Cheerio Mum, Look after yourself.

Your loving son
as ever

Bob

PS The parcel is lasting very well but by this time next week it will be looking a bit sorry for itself I bet. I was thankful for that sugar and butter.

THE DURN
PERTHSHIRE, SCOTLAND

Thursday 30th April 1942

Dear Mum, & all

I'm very pleased to tell you that I've passed my medical OK and am fit for flying. I start tomorrow flying. Oh boy! Am I looking forward to it. Weather here has been ideal today. Really hot as Hornchurch and no wind. I'll be getting RAF battle dress tomorrow too. Everything here (so far) is extremely decent. I have no complaints at all bar getting up at 6 o'clock and nothing to eat till 7.30 am. But that's not much to grumble at is it..?

It seems ages now since I use to bunk home from Regent's Park.

Tuesday 5th May 1942

PPS Have now got air force
battle dress. It's smashing.
Warm, comfortable and tons of
big pockets.

Dear Mum, Ken & Pop,

Received your letter Monday. Hope you are all well and happy. I am
keeping pretty fit myself. Weather hasn't been too warm and clear
for flying today but I got an hour in (so far have done one and a half
hours dual).

Somebody told me flying was easier than motoring – it's far more
complicated flying, and at first it needs terrific concentration to fly
both straight and level towards say a distant mountain top on the
horizon. I was surprised how sensitive the controls are – finger tips
only required on the joystick and only easy pressure on the rudder
bar.

Today I did climbing and gliding and a few stalls. Stalls are some
sensation – the nose of the plane is pulled right up at about 4,000
feet, and when it looses flying speed with the throttle closed the nose
suddenly drops and you seem to dive straight down, leaving your
tummy behind you. But you even get used to this in time. Of course
it is too early yet to say if I'm going to make a flyer or not. It's just
the same as people who can play football well or badly. My
instructor – a very nice fellow – a pilot officer, hasn't told me off
much so I might be OK. We'll see. I hope so, for flying must be jolly
good when you've had a bit of time at it.

The CO has told us that the air ministry doesn't want so many
pilots at present, which may mean that we stand less chance of
getting through here. Still, if I fail it will be that it just doesn't come
easy enough to me. Not for want of trying.

Do you remember 'Cobber Cain' – the Australian ace; well it took
him much longer than the average to pick up flying and solo, but he
was not suspended in those days, and look what a good pilot he
made. If you don't solo under fourteen hours (the most) you are

I'm very pleased to tell you that I've passed my medical OK, and am fit for flying.

chucked off the course – it seems daft to me. It is not always the fellows who pick the things up quickest who make the best pilots.

Oh well! We'll see. Anyway you don't want me to write nothing else but flying talk, though of course I'm naturally full with it just now. Flying makes all of us too tired to eat.

This afternoon I had a try at lawn tennis – first time really. It's not a bad game. The others went swimming in Perth, but I didn't want to risk a cold yet. Things are fairly free and easy here – it's pretty good all round. I'd like to stay here.

Tomorrow we're allowed to sleep out and have all day Thursday off. Mrs Banks wants me to go over there, to Aberdalgie (about five miles away), so I shall have a decent peaceful day with a lay in bed on Thursday. Her daughter went back Sunday night, and her husband is home now, discharged from the RAF.

I've phoned Chris again last night, and I'm so glad she's been going about with you a bit. I managed to get two more pairs of silk stockings – one for yourself and one for Chris. They cost me fourteen 'bob' but you're worth fourteen million quid so I don't mind at all. I only hope they're decent quality. At least they'll save you a couple of coupons. I'll send them as soon as I can get down to the post office.

I'm disappointed about the Silvikrin, and please ask Ken to send some as soon as he can will you? Mrs Banks has received your table-cloth OK and was extremely pleased. Thanks Mum. She gave me your letter to read.

Don't worry I shan't go dancing much, at the most once a week and probably not that. I'm only really interested at present in getting through this course and getting leave again.

Well Mum, this is all for now I think so I'll close here. Goodbye for now, look after yourself. Keep well and as happy and content as you can during these days. Remember me to Aunt Edie when you see her. Cheerio!

All my love
your loving son

Bob X X X X X X X X

PS When I saw Alice home from the dance on Saturday, her mother had a smashing supper ready and even had a pair of pyjamas in front of fire for me. But I couldn't stop.

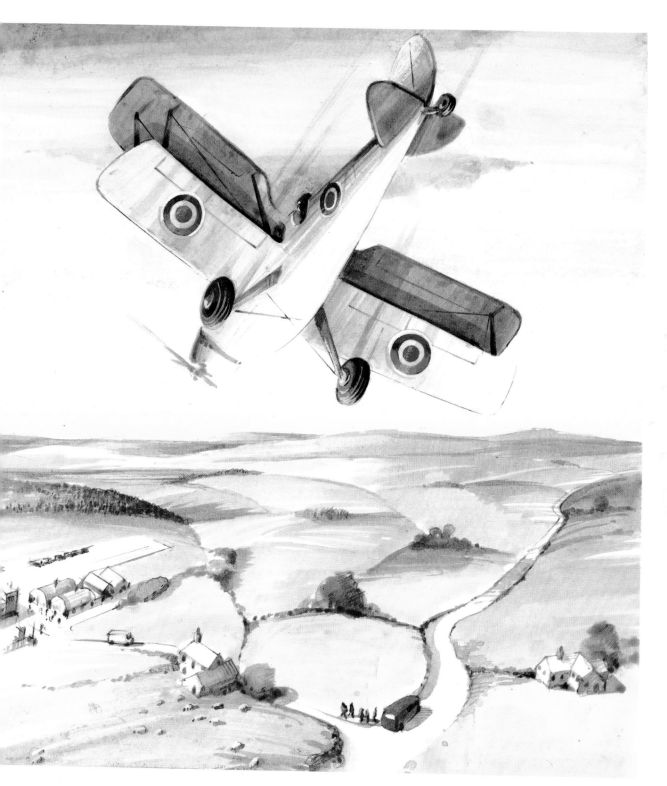

You dive straight down leaving your tummy behind!

Thursday 15th May 1942

Dear Mum, & all

…I have done only four and a quarter hours flying so far. I had a bit of bad luck on Tuesday – sprained my wrist, playing about and it stopped me flying on Wednesday. Today was called off, and I slept over at Mrs Banks' place last night and had a lovely quiet day there today. I had a lovely breakfast at 11 o'clock. Sausages, bacon, egg, scones – oh! it was like being home. Wrist is a lot better now, and I expect the MO will let me fly tomorrow. I hope so for I love it now, and I hope I pass here. You have to do twelve hours flying here before you leave. I don't know if I told you but last Saturday I was in a plane that took part in Warship Week over the Bridge of Earn. Three planes in formation, three instructors and three pupils stunted right over the hospital and village. It was smashing, I enjoyed every minute. My instructor's a decent fellow (a pilot officer)…

THE DURN
PERTHSHIRE, SCOTLAND

Sunday 24th May 1942

Dear Ken,

Thanks for the letter received Saturday. I'm glad things are going OK with you. I was surprised to hear old Stephens had gone at last. (Do you know on what job?) Anymore rises just yet? How are the girls? You don't mention any in your letter.

For myself I'm, how shall I say – strictly teetotaler at present. I've not been to any dances for the last two weeks – only flicks, an occasional walk with a girl and Thursday at Aberdalgie. Dancing fags you out too much for flying next morning.

Incidentally, I've done no flying for three days. 'B' flight has been

When I saw Alice home from the dance on Saturday her mother had a smashing supper ready and even had a pair of pyjamas in front of the fire for me.

I was in a plane that took part in Warship Week over the Bridge of Earn ... it was smashing.

out of luck with the weather lately. Scotch mist, and today rain and squalls, bugger it! So I'm a bit cheesed just now. Up to date I've done eight and a quarter hours (leaves three and three quarters to do before the CFI test). They are not concerned now whether you solo before twelve hours or not. It depends mostly on your instructor and the weather, and your luck. But I hope I have the luck to pass Flight Commander's solo test, and go solo for twenty minutes.

The Air Ministry is buggering about something awful just now – they want bomb aimers, so to fill the gap until they have sufficient outside volunteers, they are taking in a certain percentage of potential pilots. Therefore the standard required has been raised temporarily and your unlucky cuss of a brother has started at an unfortunate time. But I should know the result if the weather is OK the end of this week or beginning of next. Of course you know what I want it to be.

You'd like flying Ken – it's smashing (of course I've not had enough time at it to judge yet). I've only got to learn side slipping and steep turns on this syllabus now – the rest of the time will be on brushing up the lot.

If a posting doesn't come through for a couple of weeks and I get through I'll get a few hours solo in with a bit of luck before I get home…

THE DURN
PERTHSHIRE, SCOTLAND

29th May 1942

Dear Mum, Ken & Pop,

I'm rather pleased with myself at present Mum – I took my solo test this morning, passed OK and the Flight Commander let me go solo straight away. Oh boy! you can imagine how pleased I was. Nine hours and then solo's fairly good going for anyone really. I had the plane all to myself for ten minutes, but I did nothing daft – I was just content to take her off, circle the 'drome once and land. The landing was the best I've ever done yet. The Flight Commander watched me and a couple of instructors and everyone said I made a pip of a

The Flight Commander watched and said I made a pip of a landing.

landing. So I'm on top of the world today. The first stage is won. There remains the big test – the CFI on this course after two more hours dual instruction and then home sweet home for a bit I hope.

…Enough about flying. I had a lovely photo from Chris yesterday. I owe her a letter now and shall write to her tomorrow.

I went over Aberdalgie again yesterday and had a quiet time. The country there is wonderful now. Waterfalls, trout streams – clear and cool – lovely. Carpets of bluebells, primroses and forget-me-nots. Oh! you'd love it…

BASILDON WORKS
SOUTH TOTTENHAM
LONDON

17th June 1942

My dear Kimberley,

Once more the time has come round when we are able, through the generosity of your colleagues, to send you a postal order. I think we told you some time ago that it had become quite impossible to collect up goods so that a parcel could be prepared for you. We are sorry about this but hope you can make use of the cash.

Very glad to tell you that everything goes well in the Department. We are keeping reasonably busy in spite of continually losing both male and female workers, somehow manage to keep jogging along.

There are quite a number of people now who feel it is possible that the war will be over this year. Some of us may not agree but we all hope and pray that such may be the case and that we shall all be united together in our homes and other civil occupations before many months have passed.

No doubt you will, as soon as convenient, acknowledge receipt of this letter and enclosure.

With very best wishes from us all.

Yours sincerely

S Harrison

Letter from Bob's employer, John Dickinson.

Carpets of bluebells, primroses and forget-me-nots. Oh! you'd love it.

HEATON PARK
SELECTION BOARD, MANCHESTER

Thursday 18th June 1942

Dearest Mum, Ken & Pop,

Arrived here at 11.00 am Wednesday. Everything is first rate so far. We should know in under a week whether we are pilot, observer, air-bomber or what-not. If pilot then it will be pretty definitely an abroad posting...

HEATON PARK
SELECTION BOARD, MANCHESTER

Saturday

Dear Mum & all,

I got back here OK after a decent journey, and have delayed writing to you before as there were rumours of a posting. Well the rumours have turned out right for once – I shall be going this coming week. We don't know where or when, but I can tell you that it's pretty sure that it's not Africa for we have been given shoes and a few extra items of kit and it wasn't tropical kit. I'm very glad.

So it'll probably be Canada or America – Canada I think for certain reasons...

29th June 1942

Dear Mum, Ken & Pop,

Well it looks as though I shall be going very soon now.

I was inoculated on Sunday (the parade fixed any ideas of getting home, worst luck) and the effects are wearing off now (it affected me very little really).

Tomorrow we have a secret session and we're told when and where we are going. It should be Wednesday from here – of course we won't know when the boat sails or from what port till the very last and it's fairly certain to some place in Canada. We've got our kit all packed and have only to get paid.

Tomorrow we'll be told the exact place in say Canada, and what type of planes we'll be on to start with. Probably Canadian Tiger Moth. Some of the fellows on our posting haven't had any flying – straight from ITW so I'm very pleased for I've had some experience and have solo'd.

We should be away from England for about six months (it's a bit shorter now) which means we'll be back (if I pass that is and don't have to do another air crew course) soon after xmas – not too bad is it?

We are allowed to write to you just before we sail, and I shall cable you as soon as we arrive (anything from six – twelve days).

…I'll be OK don't worry and I'll write often and regularly and I know you'll do the same.

…Well Mum, look after yourself – not too much work and don't let people worry you with rumours about the war, or crashes – flying training is absolutely safe – its only when you take silly risks and I like living too much. I'll only take risks when I have to.

Well goodbye and God bless everybody. Look after yourselves. I promise I shall Mum.

Yours as ever

Bob X X X X X X X

June 1942

Dearest Mum & all,

Have arrived on board ship OK, and should be sailing very soon.

There's very little for me to say just now – like everyone else I'm waiting eagerly to get going as we are very cramped and the sooner we get to the other side the better.

…Tell Ken that civvy street may be boring but if the merchant navy is anything like this ship, I don't think he'd be too struck.

Well, Mum and everyone, please don't worry over me – I'll let you know as soon as we dock the other side, and then we can start writing (the air graph service has been started and that means quicker correspondence).

…Well, Mum, I'm fairly content at present – it'll be far from a pleasure cruise, but there…

On board ship bound for Canada

June 1942

Dearest Mum & all,

You will probably hear from me (by cable) before you receive this letter: they say a cable reaches England in fifteen minutes.

I'm writing this particular letter on board ship. We have done most of the journey and should be there in a couple of days. There is precious little to talk about really. The trip has been terribly boring – the amusement being practically nil, but the weather has been fair, so that we've been able to be up on deck most of the day.

Have arrived on board ship … we are very cramped.

I'll write again, as soon as I can, when we're on good old terra ferma.

Accommodation has been very cramped, but food very good. (We've had oranges, apples, cheese, onion – all Canadian I suppose.)

…I was lucky enough not to be sea-sick, but many of the fellows were really ill with it. We get 10s 2d per day when we land – food, tobacco, etc is very cheap, but things like hair-cuts are double the price in England we've been told.

…I'm hoping when I get settled there to be able to buy some civvy clothes – perhaps even a suit, and some other stuff to bring back. (That's if we're allowed to bring it back.)

Well Mum, the course should last about six months, so I'll be home early next spring (perhaps even before) if I pass.

…I hope everything is going OK at home – everybody well and happy as possible. You're not working too hard? I hope not. Of course I'm pretty home-sick already, but I'll get over that a bit when we land. I'm looking forward to seeing this new country, and we should get a decent time there, provided the course doesn't entail too much swotting.

Oh boy though! Like I've said many a time before – you won't get me straying far away from Hornchurch when this b——— nuisance of a war is over. There's nothing, I'm absolutely certain now, to compare with home and civvy street. Tell old Ken he'll be absolutely mad if he joins anything at his age. He can leave it for ages, though I don't suppose for a second that the war will last that long. God! I hope not.

…I'll write again as soon as I can when we're on good old terra ferma…

MONCTON, CANADA

17th July 1942

Dearest Mum & all,

I have cabled you – I hope you received it OK (if anything very important or urgent happened at home you can always cable me).

I'm feeling top of the world at present. Conditions were very poor on the boat but crossing was uneventful and all's well, etc.

It is like coming into paradise here… The people too are marvellously hospitable – some people asked some pals and me to supper last night, first night here.

It is like coming into paradise here. Food served at the camp is marvellous – all the butter, sugar, milk you want. (I'm just eating whipped cream on apple pie, banana and iced milk at a YMCA as I write). The people too are marvellously hospitable – some people asked some pals and me to supper last night, first night here. (Tell Pop there's no beer served in these parts). I wished to God you all could enjoy the advantages here: it doesn't seem fair for me to be having all this (no blackouts, etc) while you have to endure England in its present unplentiful state. Still maybe it won't be long before England is the same again.

I shall be here, in this receiving centre at Moncton, a week or more probably, but any letters will follow me to flying school. When you write mark your envelope 'transatlantic air mail' – enquire at the post office, and that will reach me much sooner although postage will be more. I'm itching to hear from you. I hope you are all well and happy. If I pass I should be home by next spring. I shall be writing a long ordinary letter immediately after this air-graph. Write often Mum, please, won't you, and we'll soon have correspondence going regularly I hope.

Yours as ever
Love

Bob X X X X

MONCTON, CANADA

Early July 1942

Dearest Mum & all,

I hope you received my cable and air-cable OK. Are you all well and happy – I hope so, for I'm having a lovely time in Moncton. As I've told you the food is marvellous and so are the billets and the people here.

Today I've been swimming and sun-bathing with Ken Robson and

Please send your letters to Miss A Irving

another pal at a place on the coast called Pont-du-Chene (twenty miles away). It's been wonderfully warm. (We got a lift easy.)

Yesterday I sent you a parcel from a big store. It should reach you in a month. Contains two pairs of silk stockings, a box of chocs and two shirts (the one with the zip is for Pop – a workshirt).

It pretty well broke me – 35/-, but I'll manage till pay-day OK and it was worth it to think of the possible pleasure you'd get. I'd like it to been a surprise but I want you to let me know if you get it OK. I shall send you another when I can.

We should be going to flying school soon, so please send any letters to this private address below and I'll get them forwarded quicker. It's some people I've met.

Miss A Irving,
186 St George St,
Moncton, Canada, NB

Well this is all just now mum. Keep well and happy for me and don't worry – I'm having a wonderful time. I only wish you could all enjoy it with me. I'd like to come back here after the war to live.

All my love
Yours as ever

Bob X X X X X X

MONCTON, CANADA

20th July 1942

Dearest Mum & all,

I have very little to say just now, but here goes. I'm still having a decent time here, but am waiting for pay day – that parcel just about broke me. Still pay should be any day now. We have been told that we'll be going to flying school soon – but it's OK, you're letters will be forwarded OK. Weather has been wonderful and I've done plenty of swimming and sun-bathing at Pont-du-Chene – twenty miles away

They are just crazy on jitter bugging here.

on the coast. I'm feeling very fit – Perthshire last January seems like a bad dream long ago now.

I'm putting on weight with all the decent grub but the heat sweats a lot of it away. I've tried their dances here, but they're crazy on jitter bugging. I've got a date tonight (with no money – but she knows I'm broke). Do you see anything of Chris – I miss her like I miss you all.

When you write, tell me if there's anything special you can't get at home and I'll do my best here. Incidentally I think you can write me air-graphs – they are cheapest and quickest – will you find out at the post office (you can use more than one sheet if you wish).

I've had another vaccination this week – that makes six vac scars. Ken Robson makes a smashing chum – he stands by you through anything, but I believe we'll be sent to different flying schools. Well Mum, keep writing and look after yourselves. God bless.

Your loving son
as ever

Bob X X X X X

MONCTON, CANADA

Thursday 7th August 1942

Dearest Mum, Ken & Pop,

I received your long waited for letter today Mum. Was I glad to hear from home. And I hope now that we'll hear from each other more often. I'm glad everything's normal – that you are all well and OK. How did the holiday go? This is the place for holiday weather – you should see the lovely tan I've got now from sun-bathing and swimming up at the beach. I'm still getting plenty of good food down my neck too, though I don't stuff as I did when I first got here. Yes, you're right – I've had a very lazy time of it this last month – completely put back all I lost through pneumonia last xmas. I only wish you could enjoy all the advantages of this country with me. But never mind, old England beats it all when things are back to normal. It's a bit too hot and dusty here for me.

I've heard nothing about flying school yet – the 'Ks' just missed the last posting. Did I tell you Ken Robson was parted from me, worse luck. Still that's the RAF all over! We may meet again when the course is over. But I should be the next to go now – I shall be glad to get going too. If I pass – oh boy! Just imagine coming back to you all with my wings up, and no more binding courses to take, and something definite to do in good old England. Keep your fingers crossed for me.

Thanks for writing to the firm for me. I sent them an air-graph myself last week.

I'm glad too that you're doing alright at work, and not over-doing it. As far as that shop goes, Mum, it's up to you and Pop. Personally I should like us to have it – we should do alright after the war with it and it'll be a sort of insurance for you and Pop I think. What does Pop say? It wants a lot of thinking over though. I wish that I was home with you for things like that. You've been doing everything for Ken and me all these years and just when we are old enough to help a b—— silly war has to get in the way! But never mind, it'll be over soon, and we can settle down again. Perhaps another car and lots of other good things.

It's good to know old Ken's still doing OK at work – I hope he'll write me often. You must know what it means to get news from you – write as often as you can – I can't get too many letters from you even if you don't think you have anything to write, just write Mum won't you?

Incidentally, I've written air-graphs to Alf Barker and Mrs Banks in Scotland – I'll send her a parcel like I sent you when I'm flush. (Have you got your's yet – I hope you didn't have to pay too much duty on it.) Don't forget if there's anything special you want just let me know. I'll be writing to Aunt Liz and Aunt Edie soon.

I've not heard from Chris yet – expecting to though. Do you see her at all. I should like to know. I'm sending you a snap in this letter of myself and a French Canadian girl I've been with since I landed almost. She's quite nice and is a good pal. I look rather untidy, but I'd just been for a swim and had dressed in a hurry.

The town at the back is Moncton. Well mum, I can't think of much more to say just now, so I'll close here I think.

Well, look after yourselves and write to me all you can, for a good half of me is still in Hornchurch with you all. I hope the raids aren't bothering you again – it's not a nice thought for me to be here in comfort when the news is full of raids on England some days. Well goodbye for now, keep happy and God bless!

Your loving son
as always

Bob X X X X X

PS Tell Pop I'd give a lot for a pint just now. Milk gets monotonous even, after a month. I drink three pints of it a day on average. It doesn't seem fair does it?

MONCTON, CANADA

Friday 13th August 1942

Dearest Mum & all,

I'm on my way out West now – first night's travel over and we're stopping at Montreal for the day before we start again.

It's a wonderful town, set in the river St Lawrence. I wished I could just get hold of you and drop you in the middle of one of their lovely stores. The marvellous stuff you can buy! I wished I had a ton of money so I could bring a lot home. But once I get flying I shall be able to save a good bit. I bought a lovely little wrist watch today for $8 (35/-), and some very fancy underclothes. Oh! how I wished you could all enjoy it with me. But when work starts again it's going to be pretty hard. Well, space is just about filled, so I'll have to say cheerio and God bless! I hope you are all well and everything's OK.

All my love
yours as ever

Bob

A reception committee made another big fuss of us.

Endless miles of corn and then the rolling prairies. They'll never starve here!

Calgary was a proper big Western town.

17th August 1942

Dearest Mum, Ken & Pop,

I arrived at flying school yesterday the 16th August. We travelled from Wednesday till Sunday – I wonder how Aunt Liz would like that – although we had two long breaks at Montreal and Calgary. (Incidentally we passed through Toronto.) At Montreal two pals and myself were invited out to lunch at a terrific hotel. It was a Lions Club dinner, and after a smashing meal one of them – an English fellow who came out here thirty years ago – took us around in his car. He also took us into a pub for a drink. He ordered quarts and honestly it was as much as me and my pals could do to walk out straight. He has given us his address.

At Winnipeg we were met by a reception committee who made another big fuss of us and a lot of Australian O/T pilots with us.

Calgary was a proper big Western town – shops full of horse harnesses, stetsons, etc, and the other usual array of stuff in plenty. I got a bit fed up with sitting still eventually, but it was some experience.

We passed through wonderful scenery: lovely forests, hundred's of miles of it; by the sides of lakes, Lake Superior alone is one thousand miles long – you could drop England in it. And you should see the endless miles of corn and then the rolling prairies. They'll never starve here.

The station I'm on now is in a prairie but you can see the Rockies and there is a small town close by – Bowden. The nearest big town is Calgary, which is ten miles away.

We have been told about the course today. It should take eight weeks at least, and it seems like very hard swotting. Still, I'll do my best. You get up at 5.30 am on one day and fly from 5.30 – 8.00 am (breakfast). Then you fly till 12.30 (dinner), after dinner you do ground subjects till 9 o'clock at night with break for tea. The next day you do ground subjects in the morning and fly in the afternoon, and you don't have to be on parade till 8.00 am.

So you can see we won't have much leisure time and what we do have we shall want for swotting and revision for coming exams. Each day is between thirteen – fifteen hours long. We get twenty-four hours off each week though and one thirty-six hours every fortnight, and I shall try to get about in the neighbourhood.

We are flying Stearman biplanes here instead of Tigers. They are faster and altogether better, so they say, and easier to pick up.

We may start tomorrow. The catering on the camp is done by civvies, and the food is first class. We only have to make our own beds as the civvies keep everything clean. No fatigues. Its grand.

Yes, it will be hard work, but in first class conditions...

BOWDEN, ALBERTA
CANADA

29th August, 1942

Dear Ken,

Thanks for the letter old chap, and any other time you feel like writing, please do won't you, for letters mean so much. I like to know what you're doing, personally, besides letters from Mum. Glad to see you liked that shirt. Anything else I can pick up for you (if I've any money). Incidentally, after that last parcel I was so broke for a week I even used soap for tooth-paste, etc. Old Ken Robson, an old pal of mine I met again kept me going till the buggers eventually paid us. If there's anything special you'd like please let me know. How's the job going, and how are the girls? I expect by the time I get back you'll have outclassed me in the Romeo business, and other necessities of life.

I did alright for myself at Moncton as far as girls go, but not so good as good old Hornchurch. I'd like to hear about meeting Dorothy – I was very interested to hear about it. What did she say and all the rest of it?

Well, I've been two weeks on the course to date and have only got in three hours. That means I've got to get sixty-seven hours in during the next six weeks (eight weeks course all told). I'm talking about flying hours, old chap, of course. Reason for this being my b—— instructor's on leave in Kansas City. He binds like hell all the time you're up, but he's a decent guy on the ground. I've tried my hand at take-offs, landings, general flying and spins, but it's early to tell whether I'm going to make it or not. The planes here are heavier and faster (biplanes). Top speed only 150 mph, but land at about 65 mph. They are old Mexican fighter type with lower powered radial engines they say. They are fine to fly though – solid, and I'll be glad to go solo on them. Then I'll get my hours in. We're having some night flying next week – I'm rather looking forward to it. But you're not allowed to do any solo night flying on this course.

I do hope I make this course for there's only one lap after it – SFTS: the largest lap. And then my wings if I'm lucky. And then home I hope (about next March I reckon if all goes well). There's plenty of ground subjects to fail on as you probably know, but you can only do your best.

Tonight for a bit of relaxation I'm thinking of trying the local dance (Innisfail, four miles away). It's a proper cow-boy style town. Unmade streets and fellows in farmer-style outfits. But plenty of smashing cars around as usual.

You'd like Canada Ken, but it's not home so it's not as good to me. Smashing scenery and sociable people.

Well Ken, apart from the little bit of flying, I've done nothing worth talking about really. I had a good train journey across Canada, and I hope to get a week's leave for a bit of 'prospecting' if I pass this course. So I hope then to be able to have something worth relating. In the meantime keep writing, won't you, even if you don't think you have much to say, like I often feel when I start to write home. Cheerio! for now, 'pal', and all the best.

Yours as ever

Bob

PS Tuesday 2nd September
Have just received another welcome letter from Mum, written on 19th August. Am answering it right away. Mail should be OK now.

10th October, 1942

…I have not heard from Chris more than twice since I've been here, but I have written very little to her and am as much to blame. I seem to have so little spare time. It's bind, bind, bind, all the time on this course.

I notice in your letter you say 'it'd be nice if you had a commission', Mum; well, it would be, but don't be disappointed if I remain without one for a time. It'll be at best another four months from now before I'll be considered for one. I'll have to do some operational flying too, and even then may never get one for ages. I hope you won't be disappointed too much if I am never offered one. A sergeant is better off financially in England.

Next step up to sergeant is flight sergeant (they wear a crown above the three stripes). That takes about six months after being made sergeant and comes through automatically. After about another year you are made Warrant Officer. His pay is very good and is considered one of the best ranks in the RAF all round. He wears officer's type uniform too. After this rank, if you haven't been offered a commission before (and the war isn't over in my case), you automatically get a commission I believe. The lowest rank in commissioned officers is pilot officer and if you get commissioned from Warrant Officer you go straight to Flying Officer, and miss the PO stage out. Well, I'll bet you are bored with all this RAF 'gen', aren't you?

I am sending two shirts for Ken, and three ties. Hope he likes them. Am only sending you a couple of pairs of stockings Mum, this time. Shall send more later. They had no size '9s' – the size I thought you'd wear. Hope these aren't too small.

You should have had that little parcel of groceries long ago now, my photos maybe, and perhaps my last parcel with undies in for you, and socks for Pop. Hope Pop's keeping OK. Looking forward to a drink with him. Looking forward to so many things to enjoy with you. Must close now. Cheerio! and God bless.

All my love, as ever,
your loving son (and brother, young Kipper) Bob

BOWDEN, ALBERTA
CANADA

October 1942

Dearest Mum & all,

I'm sorry at not having written for a week now, but last week was our ground exams, and I've never worked so hard since matric at school. And when we weren't doing exams we were flying – average of three – four hours a day now. I thought I'd wait for the result of my exams before writing. Well I got through OK. I got 85% on the whole lot – and came tenth out of about eighty fellows – not bad really, considering that armaments (.303 Browning machine gun) almost let me down; 52% – 2% scrape through. This bought me down to 85%, and stopped me possibly being in first four or five. Anyway it'll do, particularly as twenty-four blokes failed on armaments, two on signals, one on aircraft recognition and half a dozen on navigation. Which means that they got below 50% and will have to sit it again. So I was pretty lucky really.

I'm due for a check on flying by instruments only any time now (you fly under a hood and fly level, climb and turn by instruments while the instructor acts as safety pilot). I've done sixty-five hours flying all told now, and in about ten hours will be ready for check on ordinary flying and acrobatics.

First time I did loops and spins on my own I went up to 6,000 feet and don't mind admitting my pulse quickened up a bit when the top of the loop came and there was the old Rocky mountains upside down, and there was no instructor to sit in the back cockpit. But now they are becoming more or less routine, and really there's nothing in a loop.

This morning my instructor showed me how to do a half-roll off the top of a loop and slow full rolls. He flew the plane along for three or four minutes upside down while he demonstrated how the controls worked the reverse way upside down and I was off my seat hanging on my straps. It may sound a bit fearful, but there's nothing to get squeamish over really, and as long as you get enough height to start with, you've bags of time to correct any mistakes. It's great fun, and I do hope I pass my CFI test alright. Should be in about a week now. I'll let you know as soon as I take it, how I do.

I've never worked so hard since matrix at school.

Yesterday I did a cross-country solo – 160 miles there and back one and a half hours to De Winton, another drome, where a lot of old pals are stationed. It was dead easy. Plane almost flew itself there. A lovely day too – with the Rockies looking grand. Easier still coming back, three of us came back together – good fun.

…Well, Mum time is going and there doesn't seem to be much sign of this war finishing right now but it can't last much longer I'm sure, and that'll be the day. Tell Pop I'll drink him under the table at one of the Hornchurch pubs that day (at least I'll try to).

I get very home-sick at times, but I feel fit as a fiddle and in six months time if all goes well I should be on the way home I hope.

I'm glad you're all doing OK, and particularly glad to see that you're taking it easy at work (so you say). (Incidentally I've saved about £10 since I started this course; not bad for me.) Keep well too.

Well I must close here for now. Shall be writing again soon. Cheerio now and God bless!

Your loving son
as ever

Bob

PS Many happy returns to you and Ken for last month, I tried to get into a big town to send you something off but couldn't manage it. Shall try next week perhaps.

PENHOLD, ALBERTA
CANADA

Dearest Mum, Ken & Pop,

I just got back off eight days leave last night. I had a wonderful time and later if I can I shall send you some snaps my pal took of the places we went to and the things we did.

The first night we stayed at Calgary – a big town about sixty miles south of the camp and had a dance and a decent time there. Next day we went to Banff in the Rockies and stayed there four days. Honestly, I shouldn't imagine there's a more beautiful spot in the

I was off my seat, hanging on by my straps!

world. I only wish you could have seen it. Particularly Lake Louise – a lake about 5,000 feet up and surrounded by mountains. Its water was a real vivid turquoise blue, as blue as technicolour films.

We had neither of us ridden before but the second day we tried some horse-riding, and it was so good that we rode every other day of our leave. I was very sore but it was grand riding up the pony mountain trails and you soon got the knack of it. But there was very little to do in the town at nights so we went back to Calgary, stayed one night, another dance, and then went to Edmonton to those people I staying with before. And they made us very welcome, and it didn't cost us a cent. We bought her some stockings that was all. By the way I sent you another parcel from Hudson Bay Company in Edmonton. I hope you'll like it. I hope Ken will like the yellow pullover and scarf. You should get it just before xmas – they said it'll take six weeks to reach you. There was a letter from you waiting at the camp when I got back, one from John Sullivan and one from a pal out here.

I met some nice girls on leave too, especially a Syrian girl I met before in Edmonton at a dance, and I've got a fairly regular girl now in Innisfail – nearest town to the camp. Donna McGlee, her name is. She takes me home to her family for supper after dances, etc. Her mother is a Yankee. The family is Scotch. No father.

I am posted to an SFTS quite close by Innisfail and only about fifteen miles from here. Here's the address:

1331518, Lac Kimberley, A
36 SFTS, RAF,
Penhold
Alberta
Canada

36 SFTS RAF
Penhold, Alberta
Canada

Sunday 1st November (white rabbits!)

My Dear Ken,

I sent a letter off to Mum two days ago, so I haven't much fresh news. Anyhow I'll have a shot…

To start with, thanks for your letter, I'm glad to hear your job is going well – another rise ay? Believe me, civvy street beats them all.

So you've started a footer team. Give me some more 'gen' – news I mean, about it in your next letter will you. Who's in it, what position do you play, and who do you play?

Are you doing any biking these days? They don't go in for biking these days over here – distances are too great. I miss mine. But there, old man, you miss many things out here.

Well, as to flying – I passed EFTS fairly well, and now back at the grindstone at Penhold SFTS, twenty miles away from Bowden.

It's very convenient to do SFTS close to EFTS as I've flown over a lot of the surrounding country and know the rivers and landmarks, etc, so its not so easy to get lost.

The course lasts sixteen weeks, if you're not slung off before. You do 150 hours here flying. So far I've done five hours, and should with a bit of luck go solo in another two or three on these kites. They are totally different to the other planes I've flown, of course. Much faster and much bigger. I must stop writing about the planes here it's amazing how strict censorship is, though rightly so, I think really.

(Incidentally, where did you get the news about how we get back? You are right about a few of us. Your luck has to be in though). I should like to tell you more about the course. The ground subjects, like the instrument panels on these kites are a headache – it is nearly a twelve-hour day, but so long as I pass eventually I don't mind going all out on this last lap.

I've met a really nice local girl, as I said in one of my former letters – Donna her name is, but I don't have much time to see her now. Last night was first time I went out of the camp for a week. And I know some very nice people in Edmonton – a big town 100 miles away my pal and I hitch-hike to every other weekend. We shall get forty-eight hours leave every other weekend, and work all day (ie fly) the other Saturday and Sunday.

I know a very nice Syrian girl there – her name's Sue. So you see I'm glad I wasn't moved far. And there's a girl – a school teacher actually – in Crossfield fifty miles South of here I can see any time I want, and another in Calgary.

I had a smashing leave Ken, and my pal took some decent snaps of the Rockies, etc. They used to let us fly over the Rockies from here, but they had a couple of accidents through fellows acting the fool low flying and that's washed out for us.

The Rockies look wonderful from the air, and of course are

covered in snow now. We had first lot of snow about four weeks ago, and it will be here now I expect till the spring, except for their Indian summer, perhaps. But it's a dry cold and very healthy climate. Lovely weather.

Donna has promised to teach me ice skating if I get the spare time. They spend a lot of their evenings here, skating, ie when the lakes freeze up of course.

Funny thing happened the other day. A fellow was asking my pals if they knew a bloke called Kimberley, a commercial artist in civvy street. Eventually I got hold of him, but I wasn't the fellow he used to know. This other Kimberley was A G Kimberley, a commercial artist, aged twenty-one, tall but dark and lived at Sutton (Sutton Coldfield, Sutton Park) remember.

Well Ken I must stop here for now. Keep writing won't you? Incidentally I hope you like the parcel when you get it. There may be something in it you'll like.

Cheerio! all for now and God bless.

As ever, yours

Bob

PS See that Mum doesn't wear herself out at work, or worry over me.

PPS Incidentally the news about Canterbury being bombed has got me a bit worried too.

36 SFTS, RAF

PENHOLD, ALBERTA

CANADA

28th December 1942

Dearest Mum, Ken & Pop,

Well, did you all have a good xmas; I hope so? This is my first xmas away from home, and of course I missed you all. But I had a really good leave with some people I know in Edmonton. I've just got back to camp after five days at Edmonton. These people gave my pal and myself a really wonderful time – they did everything possible to make us feel at home. Our own room we had, and boy! the food. The earliest we got to bed any of the five nights was 2.00am, but we slept till midday each day, so some of the day was wasted. But in between sleeping and parties I managed to try out my ice-skates. The two boys at the house helped me round the rink, and it was great fun. Gosh! you'd have laughed – little children whizzing round and good old Bob just managing to stand up. These Canadians were born on skates I guess. The boys wanted my pal and I to try skiing and tobogganing but we didn't get time with so may parties. Yes, we had a really grand time, but I don't feel like work again. My final wings exams in ground subjects start in just over a week so I've got to swot like billyo besides extra flying time we must get in. So keep those fingers crossed for me. This will be my last exam for my wings apart from the final flying exam (wings exam). We should finish by the end of February, and then if I'm lucky enough to pass I'll probably be seeing you very soon afterwards.

I've just heard of some more fellows being thrown off the course. One fellow had only twenty-five hours to do – on a senior course to me. He passed his ground subjects very well, and then on a cross country got lost, ran out of gas, and had to force land in a field 100 miles from the drome. I don't know the full particulars of the case, but anyway he's been thrown off after doing very well all the way through and only two or three weeks probably to go. It's damned hard, and he seems to have taken it very hard. He's a transfer from the army and a sergeant too.

But anyway, this leave I've just had has been a real break, and I feel more like tackling the last phases of this course. And two months doesn't seem so long now. So mum with a bit of fair luck it won't be long now before I'm back in good old Hornchurch again. Perhaps before all the almond blossom trees bloom.

About xmas again – you should have seen the amount of people that sat down to xmas dinner at these people's home – eighteen of them – more like a wedding breakfast than xmas dinner. They had a Yankee sergeant pilot there too – a really swell fellow. He's itching to get over to England. He says he wants some action.

What did you do over xmas? I do hope you had a good time. While at one of the parties we went to I met a Canadian Army Captain who has just got back from England after three years, and he gave me all the news he could.

Well mum, I hope our mail will be better for the next two or three months – it should be. I shall send you air-graphs and letter by sea until they start sending air-mail by plane again regularly. That is best I think.

I met quite a few people from 'the old country' while on leave, and

Eighteen of us sat down to Christmas dinner.

they are very pleased to see you. They ask plenty of questions, and seem keen to have us come out here after the war's over. There's plenty of breathing space and opportunities I know, but I for one would want my family out here before I could be content. One old chap came from opposite the Woolwich Arsenal even.

Well, mum, I guess this is all the news for now. I hope you got my parcel in time for xmas, and perhaps the PO and snaps have arrived by now?

Well, I must close – lights out, look after yourselves for me. Keep those chins up, and here's hoping with all I've got for a happier new year for us all – particularly you three.

Cheerio and all my love.

Yours as ever

Bob X X X X X X X

PENHOLD, ALBERTA
CANADA

1st January, 1943

Dearest Mum & all,

Well, I sat my final exams last week after a period of solid swotting, and have passed OK (average of 80% all round). That leaves about six weeks of flying and other practical stuff before my final wings flying check. If I pass that OK, and do not get thrown off in the meantime for some stupid mistake, then I will have made it, and should be on my way back to Eastern Canada on the first stage home. The only thing that might stop me then is the possibility of being made an instructor out here (another two – three years in Canada then), but that possibility is fairly remote, I hope. God! Mum I must get thro' now and get back. It seems years ago since I was home. I wrote to Aunt Liz today. I got some aprons for you last weekend, and also two shirts for Ken. I will send them as soon as I get a few other things for you. Weather is very cold at present, thirty-two below today. You have to watch out for frost bite all the time.

Well, I must close here. Have written you longer letters and posted them last week. Cheerio.

All my love
as ever

Bob X X X X X

36 SFTS RAF
Penhold, Alberta
Canada

13th January 1943

Dear Ken,

I'm sorry old chap, I owe you letters – I hope you'll understand the way we've had our noses to the grindstones these last few weeks what with day and night flying and every spare moment for swotting. Please forgive your old sparring partner.

I believe I passed OK – have not had all results yet, and so there's only five or six weeks more flying and then wings flying exam.

Glad to see the team's still in being. I should like to see it. Or better still play for it. I remember Ernie Bright – a very nice guy. And I see you've followed the old team – W Ham, around a few places too. That's good! Give me some more 'gen' on meeting Len Goulden in your next letter. I remember him OK. How did you manage it? I don't like this '17' registration racket – it's all news to me and to my pals who I've mentioned it to. Gosh! I don't want <u>you</u> to leave the old homestead, pal.

But there's a very good chance of it being over before you are raked into it. Of course if you do have to go eventually, I know you'll make the best of it, and as to what service you go into, only you can decide that yourself, and no-one will influence you much if your mind is made up. But take your time, won't you. Promise?

The flyings' OK Ken. Shall be doing formation flying soon. That takes it out of you – quite a big strain at first. Night flying has been a piece of cake so far. No trouble with landings by day or night so far. Fellows have been dropping off all along for one reason or another. Have lost on average one in six fellows off my course here, so far. And of course there's always the chance that'll you'll be the next. They don't like you to hurt their planes. One fellow got thrown off for a taxying accident, and another for a crash night-flying the other night. Others for not being good enough at flying and ground subjects.

But accidents here are very rare indeed. I like flying, and when the war's over apart from teaching you to drive, we'll join a flying club – it should be very much cheaper, and if you want I'll teach you to fly.

That's very optimistic and high-hat from a fellow who's not even got his wings yet, but I'm hoping.

I fly dual with a pal sometimes, instead of solo with an instructor, for bombing practice or cross-country flights (about 300 miles), and we have some fun. We don't do anything stupid – it's not worth it – it's so easy to get thrown off the course without asking for it, but it's great to fly with another fellow like yourself.

I've started on ice-skating now, oh boy! it's not easy. You'd die of laughter if you saw me. A crowd of Canadian boys and girls helped me around on leave at a rink. But we have our own rink here at camp, and after the second attempt I actually managed to get from one side to the other on my feet and not on my arse. It's good fun. I'd like to have a go at this skiing racket too, and if we have any more weekend passes, I shall try to get up into the Rockies to Banff and have a try at it. (Of course it'll be gentle slopes at first for old Bob, you bet!)

I guess if Mum reads this letter she'll be a bit worried – thinking I'm deliberately trying to break my neck. Tell her not to worry I value it too much, and want it for good old civvy street again when this stupid interval of war has passed. Boy! Ken, we'll celebrate ay! that day.

I must close here. Keep writing and I'll answer more promptly in future. How's Mr Stephen these days. And how about your girlfriends. Send me a snap of the special one, old chap, will you.

Cheerio.

Love, you old blighter

Bob

PS Can you tell me anything of Chris?

I managed to try out my ice-skates… it was great fun. Gosh you'd have laughed…

36 SFTS RAF
Penhold, Alberta
Canada

14th January 1943

Dearest Mum, Ken & Pop,

I'm afraid I haven't any fresh news for you – I wrote to Ken today (our Ken I mean of course), but I received another letter from you today, and I wanted to answer it right away.

I'm glad to see you're all keeping fit still – keep up the good work. I, like yourself, get quite a few letters that have taken a long time, but mail is definitely better these last few weeks, thank goodness. The one I got today was dated 20th December.

I'm sorry about Billy going, and can understand how Aunt L feels, but I'm still more concerned over Ken having to register in May. He seems keen on the navy (he says <u>Merchant Navy</u> in his last letter). If he wants that, well, he'll have it I guess, and he'll be discontented in any other service. Anyway he will long for civvy street in any racket – anyone with any sensitivity would, and Ken is far from thick-skinned. But if he does have to join something before the war's over, I know he'll do OK. He's a popular fellow I've noticed with the others around our place, and he'll be the same with any bunch. I know nothing about the navy, I'm afraid, but I know its a tough job to take on. It's just up to himself, and he's too level headed to need much advice.

Of course a safe job would be in one of the RAF ground jobs, and he'd probably stay in England until the war's over, and he would learn a trade. If he considers this, the best trade to get into so far as I can see and by 'gen' I've picked up from re-musters to air-crew from ground staff is a 'fitter'.

Now a fitter is a damned good trade. He'd learn all there is to know about aero engines and planes in general – rigging airframes – oh! the lot. A fitter is a valuable guy. Promotion is not so quick as air-crew, but neither is the merchant navy. And there's not the slightest doubt that planes are the transport of tomorrow, and it'll be a really fine second string to his bow in civvy street. And of course he'd be able to take a car or motor-bike to bits in the dark. And if he gets fed up with that he could re-muster to air-crew later. That would take time though (perhaps a year or more to get re-mustering through).

Another good job is fitter armourer. Is he keen on a pilot's job? He'd get on the course ever so easy if he wanted, and of course I'll help him all I can. Or does he fancy other air-crew jobs – bomb-aimer (same pay as pilot) or observer (same pay too)? Let me know what he thinks about it. It's best if he talks about it in one of his future letters.

If he wants a pilot's course he wants to volunteer about a month before he has to register (like I did remember)? It's no doubt a worrying course, and I wouldn't advise anyone to take it on without a good think over whether the goal is good enough for the effort. But anything worth getting usually takes some getting, I guess.

Of course if he wanted a fitter's job, a course would have to be taken just the same, but it shouldn't be very bad, and he'd learn a hell of a lot of useful stuff. See how you feel about it Ken … Jack Tilley could help you on a course like that better than me. (How's he doing, incidentally.)

So Doris is getting married in February? I wonder if I'll be home in time, if I pass. I don't think so. Soon after maybe.

I'm not sure, as I said, yet whether I passed all my ground school exams last week – another two results to hear. But I'm pretty certain of those too.

Flying is going OK. (Touch wood.) Did some formation flying today. I like it, but you have to be on your toes all the time you're formatting. I really feel by now that I can fly a bit, and the end of the course isn't too far off – but I've a lot to learn yet. I'll say.

So you had a xmas card from Dorothy. I had one from Christine.

I shall send some cosmetics to Aunt Edie if I can, but I want to send something to you, Aunt L and Mrs Banks if I can, too. Just think in under two months I may be getting sergeant's pay, and have those blessed wings at last.

Sorry to hear about Uncle Jim having to probably join up soon. He's a nice fellow, and too settled in civvy street I should think to join any other racket.

I may be wrong but I class himself, Ken, and myself all in the same class as far as uniform would suit us really. The RAF's OK, but how I long for a civvy suit. How's my brown suit going. Has old Ken left any of it for me. Glad to hear old Paddy is OK.

Heard anything of John (I must write to him soon) or Alf Barker. Well, I must close again.

Cheerio for now, and all my love.

Your loving son
as ever

Bob X X X X X X X X

PS Thanks for Ken's (Walsall) address. I shall use it very soon.

PPS Have definitely passed my exams OK. Average on the lot about 80%. Good enough.

PENHOLD, ALBERTA
CANADA

7th February, 1943

Dearest Mum, Ken & Pop,

Well, how are you – still keeping well I hope? I'm keeping very fit, but I'm afraid I'm very short of news at present.

We've just had a decent spell of good weather and have been flying hard in a futile attempt to bring our flying hours up to schedule. But we are not very far behind now and should pass out of here in just about a month. My flying's going OK and it won't be long before I've done 200 hours. I've finished my night flying here.

I have done plenty of cross-country flights of late – quite often 300 miles and more, each one. It's best fun when another pupil comes along as navigator. I like formation flying exceptionally well, tho' it needs a lot of concentration, especially at first.

Provided I don't make any silly mistakes in the meantime (stupid ones I mean), and do OK on my wings test, I should pass now: after all they've spent more than the average £3000 on my training, but planes cost more than that and they're not going to take any chances on you, especially if you eventually have a crew with you. I hope, of course, as I always have, to get on to fighters – single engine or twins, if I get through here, but you can only be recommended here and you don't know for sure what you'll go on till you get to OTU (Operational Training Unit). This last course (OTU) before actual operations lasts several months.

Ken asked me to give him my impressions of the trip over here. Well, Ken, you wouldn't have to put up with the conditions on a troop transport in the merchant navy, naturally, so an account if I could give it, would be hardly fair on the merchant navy. And I was only on board ship several days.

But I must say I was terribly bored and fed up at the end. Was I glad when we docked. It wasn't a rough crossing, but a good third of the fellows were sick and they were ill. Food was good tho', and tobacco very cheap. No sir, I wouldn't join up with a sea-going racket, unless I spent at least one day in seven on dry land. No girls Ken!

But, as I've said, I don't know sufficient of the existence to judge it, so I'm afraid I can't be any help to you. Can't you get some information out of Eddie Gill, or better still from some guy actually in the merchant navy. I definitely wouldn't join it till you get some sound advice from someone in it, Ken. It won't be for a few days you know, if you do have to join up. And how about Pop – he was in it.

War news is looking every day more bright isn't it, thank goodness. I sincerely hope there's been no more raids of late. The 'bomber boys' are pushing the 'fighter boys' in the shade of late aren't they? You have to be a more accurate pilot than a fighter, tho' most people think more of the latter type. But the fighter fellow has to be a bit madder usually, I guess. He just 'hams the kite' about.

We have a blizzard on at the moment – more damned snow but I hope it clears so as we can get on with flying in the morning.

Just one month now, and if I'm lucky those wings and sergeant's pay. Sergeant Kimberley, sounds alright doesn't it? So keep those fingers crossed a little longer Mum.

Am writing to Aunt Pearl tonight. Well, I must close now – have completely run out of news. Please remember me to everyone – especially Aunt Liz. Shall write again very soon.

Cheerio and God bless

Yours as ever

Bob X X X X X X

22nd February 1943

Dearest Mum, Ken & Pop,

As usual I haven't a lot of news for you, but here goes anyway...

How is everybody, first; well I hope. I hope you're still taking it easy at work Mum; remember you promised me that and how's Pop and Ken doing too?

I sent you an air-graph to say I'd passed my final wings flying test OK, didn't I? I also had a wings flying test after that on blind flying (ie just off instruments) and coped OK.

So all the exams and tests are over at last, and all passed OK thank God! I've only another fifteen hours flying to do now on this course, and provided I do nothing stupid on these last fifteen hours (ie about four days flying usually), then I'll be getting my wings on March 5th (Friday week).

Until that day I shan't know definitely whether I'll be coming home after March 5th, or being kept out here as instructor or on a special course. I should get some idea from an interview with our CO tomorrow – a Group Captain – a rather awe-inspiring rank to a mere LAC like myself. He sometimes tells you what you will probably do in the future. I shall know definitely on March 5th. I believe my instructor has recommended me for fighters (what I wanted) and twin-engined fighters preferably. Of course that is just a recommendation and if they want so many bomber pilots when I get back home then I'll be trained at an OTU for bomber pilots and not fighters. It's just luck mostly.

I did three hours solid instrument flying yesterday and believe me it takes some concentration to keep a steady height, air speed and course for three hours almost right off. Your mind goes fuzzy at the end and at times you swear you are turning to port or starboard when your instruments say you are on a straight course.

At the end of this instrument flying endurance test you have to land her to see if your judgement has suffered. I managed a honey of a landing – couldn't have been better. In fact my landings have been tops – at least the last dozen have been practically all good three-pointers. My flying has improved tremendously over the last three weeks.

If you showed any signs of going hay-wire on this test (it's a hell of a temptation not to do a steep turn to break the spell) then that would go against you as a pilot suitable for long operational trips, and it might decide your future as an instructor instead. My Wings Instrument flying check was above average I know. My final general wings test too was satisfactory too, I believe, though as usual on tests I made mistakes I wouldn't have done on normal flying. I haven't the temperament for exams – I believe I worry too much. Anyway I've passed OK, and even if I don't get a commission, I'll at last get my wings and sergeant's stripes a week on Friday (touch wood!). I also had an altitude test the other week – you fly above a height where you should use oxygen, and after a few manoeuvres blind flying your instructor sees if you show any ill effects. You don't stop there very long of course. I was perfectly OK.

I've not been out of camp for a fortnight – flew till late last Saturday, but if we finish our hours by Friday we may get leave till wings parade on the following Friday. I think I shall go to Edmonton to some friends there, if we are lucky – depends on the weather. There I should be able to get a parcel ready for you. When I do (if I do) get my sergeant's stripes I should have about $100 back pay to draw, and that'll help buy some stuff to bring home. We should get some leave at the end of the course (Wings Parade) and are issued with tickets and dough and make our own way back across Canada to Moncton. Should be good. Be able to stay at Montreal then, and a few other places on the way back. Pity the Rockies are not east of here instead of a bit further west. I've not had a lot of opportunity to see Canada really so far. (Don't want that opportunity as an instructor, but if I'm unlucky then we'll have to make the best of it).

Had some glorious weather lately – spring can't be far off.

I'm glad that I'll probably be home long before Ken has to register (May isn't it?) Then we can see what will be best for him.

He seems to have definite opinions on the subject. The merchant navy seems a tough job with little thanks to me. Does he realise, do you Ken old chap? That all the time you're afloat you'll have the thought of submarines at the back of your mind. There are few other war jobs with a fear so constant as this, surely? But I guess he'll decide in the end. I would if I were him.

I was sorry to hear about Ken (Walsall) and Vera. She has been unlucky. They owe me a letter – two in fact. Have written to Aunt Pearl a few weeks ago.

How did Doris's wedding go?

Have you any news for me of Dorothy, Chris, Bill Hearn, Alf Barker, Chas, Gill or anyone else. You said Jim Hannaford was coming out here – is he on a pilot's course then? I thought he was taking an air gunner's course.

Well I'm afraid that's all for a bit Mum. Shall send you a wire as soon (if) as I get my wings, and I'll tell you if I'll be staying out here or coming back. There's more chance of coming back thank goodness, but it doesn't pay to make up your mind in the RAF as you realise. Cheerio! for now and all my love to you.

Yours as ever

Bob X X X X X X X

PS Have done five more hours flying today – that leaves only a minimum of ten now to do. Must watch out for swollen heads and carelessness at this stage. I know my flying is pretty good for the time I've been flying, but there's bags of room for improvement, and each of those bags are very large ones. It's like sketching, you are never satisfied with your standard of efficiency.

PPS Received three letters at once from you today. My lucky day. Dated (1) 20th January, (2) 1st January and one other. Shall answer them very soon.

CHARLOTTETOWN, PEI
CANADA

2nd March 1943

Dearest Mum & all,

Well did you get my cables OK? I bet you're as bitterly disappointed as I was that I shan't be home for at least another two months. Naturally I was very pleased to get my wings and sergeant's stripes at long last, but news that I was to go on this further course in Canada almost made me forget to be grateful. I have got over the first keen pangs of disappointment now and am on leave, however. Things look a bit brighter. I'm trying to write on a train. Should be in

Toronto in the morning. Travelled down to Calgary on Saturday and stayed over night. Met a very nice girl at a dance and was sorry to leave her on Sunday. Have been travelling since Sunday night. Have had jolly good food and decent sleeping berths, but shall be glad to get off the train. Bored stiff.

I am with two fellows who'll be on my course at Charlottetown. Don't known them too well, but we'll get along OK. Been once again split up from my special pals – they're on their way to Moncton and then England perhaps (very probably). One of these fellows knows people in Toronto and the other people in New York. We have nearly two weeks before we have to report to Prince Edward Island (PEI for short) so we shall go down to New York for a few days. Am looking forward to seeing it. Bet it's not as good as good old London though. It's about 500 miles I think from Toronto – a comparatively short distance over here.

Now about this special course. I can't tell you a lot about it as censorship stops as much as possible. It should take just over two months and I'll be starting in the second week in March probably. We've seen the syllabus, it's staggering. It seems much harder work than the pilot's course. It is mostly navigation, and other subjects such as battleship formation and ship recognition in addition to aircraft recognition. It is almost equivalent to a navigation course I should think. It'll take me all my time and swotting to get through for my navigation's none too good. Only the best fellows apparently go on this course so I should be pleased I guess. But I'm tired of courses – they're such a damned worry. Another disadvantage is that the other four fellows going with me from Penhold to Charlottetown all have commissions. I beat some of these fellows on ground subjects and was one of the five out of the whole course to get above average assessment on my flying. My instructor told some of the other fellows that I finished up his best pupil, but these other fellows got better discipline marks and had been to public schools mostly. But commissions though nice to have are not essential, and there's always opportunities to get one later on. At the end of this course I should be a specialised pilot and the qualification will always be helpful I believe.

Some fellows on passing out of this course go straight home by boat like my pals did or will do soon maybe, but the majority of us who pass it will probably help fly a plane home (second pilot to a Ferry Command pilot perhaps). But first, in that case, you have to have instruction on that type of plane – an OTU really I guess which means that you can go straight on to operational trips when you get back to England (after leave of course). That should take another two months.

Now all this information is stuff I've just picked up and is not definite but it should be near enough correct. As soon as I get the real 'gen' at Charlottetown I'll let you know of course if I can. So there are three alternatives as far as I see at present:

1 Just over two months course and then wait for a boat which shouldn't be too long.
2 Two months course, then an OTU of about two months and then either wait for a boat or more likely fly home which would be grand.
3 Failing the course in which case they could keep me out here as pilot on a Canadian Command (run by the RAF).

No 3 is the one I must avoid, so its almost like working for wings again. But we must grin and bear it Mum. I know that you want me home as much as I want to get back, and I ache to get back. But I'm lucky to be in Canada and not in the East somewhere. You do know that I'm safe at least. I wished I could get home before Ken has to register. I may do yet though. I must put my back into it then.

I shall be paid as sergeant $105 a month – less your allotment which makes it $98 – almost £6 a week and clothes, food and housing. Not bad ay? It'll be 13s 6d a day in England £4 14s 6d a week isn't it? I haven't increased the allotment but let me know if you wish it increased. One thing about being over here a bit longer is that I'll be able to send you more parcels. But gosh! will I be glad to get back. I long for the day now, and intend to make the most of this leave so as I can start this course feeling fresh. So keep your fingers crossed for me still. I've got the most important thing, my wings, and now I've got to work to get home. My pal who is going straight back to Moncton from Penhold, and who wanted and volunteered for this course I'll be going on, has promised to post some snaps of me he took as soon as he lands in England but I'll get some more taken and send them to you right away.

I sent you an air-graph before I left Penhold and shall send you more letters and cards whilst on this leave. This is all for now, except to hope that you're all well. Please try not to feel too badly about my not coming home right after getting my wings. I'm trying; perhaps in a few months – summer instead of spring I'll be back. God! I hope so as soon as possible.

Cheerio for now, that drink will have to wait a little longer Pop.

All my love
everybit
as ever

Yours Bob X X X X X

PS Although Mum it is hard on us at the moment that I'm not coming home right away, in the long run it'll probably be best for me to have this extra course at the back of me, and I know for a fact that the fellows are hanging around a long time in Moncton and may even be posted to Canadian jobs.

Please excuse scribble – train swaying all the time.

Love Bob

PPS Incidentally the news about Canterbury being bombed has got me a bit worried too.

CHARLOTTETOWN
PEI, CANADA

30th March, 1943

Dearest Mum, Pop & Ken,

I sent you off an air-graph yesterday, but I received two letters today from you. I was pleased to see them in the rack at lunchtime, as you realise letters mean so much. One had been forwarded on from Penhold. It was dated 14th February. The other came directly here and was only written on the 3rd of this month. That's good as all future mail from you will not be delayed by going across Canada to

It was quite a big moment on wings parade when the Group Captain stuck them on my tunic. And what a relief!

Penhold in the west and back here. You see in Charlottetown I am almost halfway home. Canada is a big place. Too damned big!

I'm so glad you had a good time at Doris's wedding. How I wished I could have been there. I hope she's going to be very happy.

I wonder who the Valentine is from. I had one from a Canadian girl too. Who could it have been in England. I bet you 'pooh-poohed' it. I can imagine the way you'd look at it and laugh, Mum.

God! I get such a longing at times to see your faces again. I never thought home-sickness could be such an ache – it's almost a little physical pain if you sit and day-dream. There's not an hour goes by, except when I'm flying or working hard on the ground part of this course that I don't remember something that happens back home. But I console myself with the thought that in two months from now I may be on my way back.

...You say maybe I'll get a commission. If I come home straight after this course, or even a few months after, I shall be sergeant still, or perhaps a flight sergeant pilot if I stay out here for OTU like I explained in earlier letters.

When I get back to England and have had some time on operations then there is a good chance – particularly as I'll have this course I'm doing now (if I pass) to help get me a recommendation for one.

If I do pass this course, I'll hold a second-class navigation certificate in addition to being a pilot. Though it's not a usual observer's course. As I've told you I can't say much about it as it is considered secret. Sufficient to say I should be in the best flying branch of the RAF at the end of it (Coastal Command). And what you'll like about it is that in this particular branch the casualty list has been very low indeed. I wanted just plain Fighter Command but at present it doesn't seem likely for me.

Yes, I received Ken's congratulation cable first day here. Thanks for it. Thanks a lot. I didn't feel very excited on the whole about getting my wings, as before in addition to becoming pilot it meant I'd be on my way back. But I'll be better off in the long run for these extra weeks out here on this extra course (if I pass). But I must admit it was quite a big moment on wings parade when the Group Captain stuck them on my tunic. And what a relief...

Thursday 17th June 1943

Dearest Mum, & all,

I received your letter of the 6th June today. That's very good going isn't it? Only eleven days. Funnily enough I get mail much better from England since I've been here than when I was 3000 miles nearer to you in Charlottetown. I do hope it's not just a flash in the pan and that it keeps up till September. Glad to hear you are all AI, tho' I don't suppose for a minute that you'd tell me if you were otherwise would you? (Don't take offence at that – you know what I mean.)

Glad you received Ken's parcel OK. I hope he liked it alright. So you gave Chris a pair of stockings I sent. That's good Mum. I'm glad you seem such good pals. Glad she comes round a lot. You think she is eager to see me again? That's good too. Naturally I want to see her too.

Pay day was yesterday and I'm waiting for the opportunity to get out early to Victoria to send you some cosmetics and a razor for Ken. I also promised to send John Sullivan some shirts and ties. On top of that I want to order a civvy suit and that'll cost me up to about $40 – that's about £9 – clothes are pretty expensive here. Wages are high compared to England but some things like clothing are very expensive. But I want to get a civvy suit before I get back as I guess they are equally expensive and less selection in England.

When the weather's good here, and it usually is grand, it is a pretty nice place, but there's little to do when the weather's poor for Victoria is a good way off and we are flying now till 8.00 pm officially.

We are flying half days at present and ground school for the rest of the day. If we fly in the morning then we start at 7.00 am. Night flying too. I did my first solo on the operational planes here about four or five days ago. It was something of the same feeling as my first solo on the little old Tiger Moth back in Scotland – remember? I must say I like these planes very much, they're a pleasure to fly. But I'm going to take things very steady as regards low flying, etc until I've had plenty of time on them and can really handle them. And then I'll still take as few risks as possible. If I am to have any accident, and

I shouldn't as most accidents until you are in actual combat are caused through taking unnecessary risks, then I want to have those accidents in England, not here.

But there, I'm getting morbid. I know you worry over me, and I want to assure you Mum that I take things easy. There's no sense in asking for it. And besides that I've got crew to worry over soon, and it wouldn't be fair to risk their necks unnecessarily. They are great fellows and we'll be posted together if we all pass. To England I mean. I'll probably lose the Aussie air-gunners as I told you if I go on to a twin-engine fighter-type when we do get to England, and just keep my observer, but the Aussies will be posted with me to begin with and I'd like to bring them down home if it's possible. Of course I want to come home first on my own, and you can tell me then if they can come along for a day, perhaps longer. You know how lonely they'll be in a strange town and if they come to London they'll probably spend all their money in the West End and get b—— all satisfaction for it.

...It will be wonderful to live there [Queen Charlotte Islands] in the summer if you had a boat to get to Vancouver. It would be old Ken's heaven. It's certainly mine. I wish you had been there to see it with me. Yes, money can do quite a lot, I guess. Seattle, in the States is no farther than Vancouver from Victoria. Please excuse these scribblings, they are stuff that might be of use to the enemy perhaps. Anyway it's best to be careful. Victoria is quite a way from here but you can get there fairly easily by bus. We get no rest days, as far as I know at present. That's bad, but there are bound to be 'stand-off' periods in which we can go to Victoria, sun-bathe and swim in the sea very nearby. We get two forty-eight-hour passes in the time here. Not much really, when I believe we work everyday. I'll probably go to Seattle or Portland in the States. Only a six-hour boat trip.

We start flying on Wednesday and for a time I'll be having a few hours 'refresher' course on the planes I flew at SFTS, besides 'starting in' on the 'real' planes here. I flew the same planes as Ron Leggo at SFTS, and I'll never regret it as they say they are about the most difficult trainer, and will stand me in good stead on operational types here and in England.

Very few guys fail here. If they do so they go to another OTU on to easier planes, usually. Yes, so long as they don't get any new ideas and stick to their usual programme, I'll be definitely coming home in September (touch wood!). But as you and I have been disappointed so often already, don't absolutely count on it in case I'm kept in Canada or sent elsewhere.

I wrote cards to Mrs Banks, Aunt Edie and Aunt Liz also a letter to Mrs Banks and one to my boss at JDS. I used up some of the most tiring part of the train journey with letter writing.

Just had lunch. Wasn't too bad, but am glad you can get really good meals outside when you have the time – RAF cooking!

I shall send you some cosmetics next time I can get into town.

Well Mum, I guess this is about all for now. I'm keeping well. Haven't had one day's illness since I've been in Canada. No colds (touch wood).

I hope you are all well and as happy as can be. Tell Ken to hold his horses about the navy till I get back. I should be home before his birthday. So keep your fingers crossed for me for another few months. (They must be aching by now, Mum ay?)

Well, I'll close now. Time to get started on drawing parachutes, etc, and all the usual preliminary 'pep' talk by the CO and chief instructors.

Goodbye for a little while and here's to September.

All my love
yours as ever

Bob X X X X X

HARROGATE
YORKSHIRE

Tuesday 12th October 1943

Dearest Mum & Pop,

Here I am again back in the old groove, and missing my cup of tea in bed, and endless cups of tea all day. This last leave has made me realise all the more how much I want to get back to civvy street.

You certainly gave me a lovely time Mum. It's only when you get

I'm missing my cup of tea in bed.

back off leave and have time to think that you fully appreciate how good a time you have had really.

My train was late getting in to Harrogate and we started a hashed-up training programme today – no flying of course. Have got swimming in the morning. Am back in the same room I had at the Majestic with my pals. One has a radio being repaired so it's not too bad.

All I'm looking forward to is next leave. If Chris comes up now and again time won't seem so long. It'll be something to look forward to anyway.

I'm looking round for an engagement ring, but will probably wait till I can get to London on my next leave.

I expect you're waiting for Ken to come home now. I very much doubt if I can get a '48' to see him, but will try and let you know result. How is he? I'm writing him tomorrow. Have got his address. I've still got great hopes for that life of mine soon. Remember – you and Pop in Aunt Edie's shop and Chris and myself next door, or at least very near, either in a shop or house and both old Ken and myself in civvy street. I've absolutely no interest in the RAF now. I'm not even greatly interested in flying any longer. I want a quiet settled existence soon with a fairly secure future. Married, you very near, a car and…oh! you know what I want out of life.

I met an old pal of mine here. My first chum in the RAF, I was chums with him at Babbacombe and Newquay. He got his wings fifteen months ago, got married and three months after had a crash. His arms and back are badly burned but he's perfectly OK again though he suffered a lot. He was so badly upset – he never got on to operational flying, it happened at an OTU – that they took him off flying for good and he's a 'link' instructor now.

I'm looking round for an engagement ring.

His wife lives with him at Harrogate and they seem to manage OK. Very well in fact. Saved £300 in a year. She works here but they managed OK when Eric was at OTU, and she was with him, and not working. Am going to his place one evening next week, and shall take Chris along there when she comes (if I don't get home).

I've found a decent little hotel she can stay at in a little place called Knaresbro' – fifteen minutes' bus ride from here, and if she comes to Harrogate Saturday morning I can be with her Saturday and Sunday alright.

If I don't get leave next week (and probably shan't – in fact chances of leave until I've been posted away from here, and done another course, don't look very good) and Chris does come up here next weekend, would you get her to bring me my pipe (at Alf Barker's) a tin of pipe tobacco I left on the sideboard, my black gloves and some drawing stuff that Ken could sort out for me: a few pots of poster colour, watercolours, brushes, drawing instruments and set-square (in book case). It's a lot to ask her to bring, but I'd like it if possible and hope she doesn't mind.

I'll tell her about it in a letter I'll write after this. Thanks for sending that letter on from Christine's mother. She seems all in favour of our getting engaged. Seems a nice person.

Well Mum, I'll have to close here. I hope you're taking it pretty lazy at home and not rushing around for other people like you did for me. Look after yourself. Hope Pop is OK too.

Cheerio for now and all my love.

Your loving son
as ever

Bob X X X X X X X

29th October 1943

Dearest Mum & Pop,

I received a letter from you this morning. It was written Wednesday, posted Thursday and I got it Friday.

I also received a letter from Chris today. These two letters were the first I'd received from home since I left, and I must admit after waiting on two posts a day my disappointment grew quite big.

But I guess I'm moaning again already, forgive me. I realise you, Mum, must be pretty busy, and old Ken being home till Wednesday didn't help you as far as spare time went I guess.

…So you're back at work again. Please don't work too hard, Mum. Promise? Yes I'll bet work didn't go down too well first day back. It never does.

I believe by her letter that Chris'll be here tomorrow. I hope so – it's the next best to being home. I have missed her of course, and am looking forward a great deal to seeing her.

I know it's only a week since I was home but time goes very slowly here. I shall be glad to be posted in many ways – now – get on with some flying and the time to my next leave will go much quicker and things will be more interesting.

…I ache to be home all the same I'm afraid, and will be glad to get flying again to occupy my thoughts.

But don't worry, Mum let me say once more that it'll not be long now before you have both Ken and I back home for good.

Remember that song that says something about 'wishing will make it come true' – well we have wished hard enough and will continue to do so I guess until we get our wish.

Keep your chin up, and don't worry too much if you can't manage it over any raids. I wish I could be with you when the blasted things are on, although I could do little to help of course.

Well, goodbye for a little while.

Your loving son
as ever

Bob X X X X X X

Thursday night 4th November 1943

Dearest Mum & Pop,

I have settled down a bit at this station now, so I can write you a short letter – I have written you once but have not heard from you, tho' Chris in her letter said you were writing Tuesday I believe. Still I'll hear soon.

I haven't a lot more to say about the place than before except for one rather distressing thing that I'll come to later in this letter.

Food is the best I've had since I joined the service (leaves excepted of course). Mess is jolly good, and WAAFS give us first-class service.

The working day is long 8.00am – 6.00pm and practically no days off. But there'll be plenty of hanging around in crew rooms when weather is too bad to fly. Had lectures today. Start flying tomorrow.

Got my wish at last – fighters (long range) which I'll fly on operations, but we have a little time on slower planes with instructors first, so don't worry.

We ride round camp on bikes instead of walking – it's so dispersed. So please send bike clips with Chris if she comes up here next week.

You'd laugh if you saw my funny 'old iron'. Sounds like a bag of nails. Tell Ken that I'll be over his place quite often in the near future – probably a lot after a few weeks time. He'll probably recognise the type of plane as he did an aircraft recognition course and perhaps remembers the name of the 'kite'. I was hoping to get used to them here, but if he sees one of the 'kites' from here (mine or another guy's) tell him not to tell anyone where it's from.

We've been issued with plenty of extra equipment here – including white sweaters and whistles.

I've not been out of camp yet since arrival as there has been plenty to do, and will be for quite a time I expect. Course doesn't appear too strenuous, but practically no time off. Now in about a month's time I may get home on a forty-eight-hour pass, but it is very slim chance. Also at xmas I may get a day or two. If not, I'm afraid it will mean

Tell Ken I'll be over his place quite often in the near future – probably a lot after a few weeks time.

January or February (depending on state of weather) till I'm through here and home on leave.

Now this leave at end of this place should be at least two weeks, but it depends (and now comes something I've been trying to keep away from you till the last). It depends on whether I'm to go overseas after leave or stay in England. It'll be indefinite leave until they decide and I'm wanted probably.

Now this business overseas – I knew when I got back to England I may soon be leaving again, but hoped I may stay, so didn't say much to you, as I know how you feel (and probably worse) – same as me. But I was told with the rather few blokes here with me that we were more likely to go overseas than stay here after we were through here. When we've finished here we are ready for operations – here or overseas. I wanted to keep this from you, but then thought it wisest to break the news gradually.

Now there is a chance of staying but even if I do go it shouldn't be for so long as the time in Canada. I'll probably only have to do one tour of operations, honestly, and then be posted back to England on a cushy 'rest job' – bags of leave and not much work.

I will be away, (if I go) six months to a year. Of course it may be much longer or shorter, but it shouldn't be according to 'gen' I've collected, from pretty reliable people.

And there are far fewer casualties in the Middle and Far East than on home-based squadrons. Far fewer – honest again. And as far as actual distances go I don't expect to be as far away from you as I was five months ago.

Gosh! Mum, I hate to do this to you, but cannot do anything about it – if I do have to go, and it'll only be because I have to (I'll not volunteer don't worry) it'll not be all that long and I'll be OK.

All I hope is that Ken doesn't leave England if I do. Hope he never does. If only I could arrange things my way you'd not have another worry – however small in the rest of your life and he and I'd be in civvy street.

But there it is, I might go and probably shall.

But it's some time yet – I may be home or in England a few months after I finish here and anything may happen to keep me here.

I still don't know whether I did right telling you, as I could have saved you anxiety till January, but I thought it best to tell you exactly how things are for me right now.

I've told Chris, I'm terribly glad you have her there now, when there's the chance of Ken and I being away for a long time, for I guess by now she's almost like a daughter for you, and company when Pop's not with you. How is he? Well I hope. Hope we can have a beer or two together this xmas morning Pop!

Now if I go overseas Mum sometime next year you mustn't forget that I might just as easily be stationed in northern Scotland or Ireland and then only see you once in three or six months and be operating in a more dangerous theatre of war.

I know I'm trying to cheer you up, I'm nothing but a bloody nuisance and worry for you, am I my dear Mum.

If I ever have any children I hope they're girls in case of another war. But I can't help it. I may not go and if I do it'll not be for long and I'll soon be back with silk stockings, cosmetics, etc, from another part of the world.

How's old Ken? We may finish our courses about same time and get leave together.

Impossible to get leave only on very compassionate grounds from here, unless they see fit to let you go for their convenience.

Don't forget, try not to worry over me. I'll be very careful here, and I may not go overseas. If I do we'll make the best of it.

Don't work too hard and take it easy all round, please Mum.

All my love
and God bless!
your loving son

as ever Bob X X X X X X X

CROSBY-ON-EDEN
CARLISLE

Sunday 21st November 1943

Dearest Mum & Pop,

I believe you owe me a letter Mum, but it doesn't matter – here goes again on my part, and anyway there'll probably be a letter for me from you tomorrow.

Well how are you both – keeping fit? I'm OK myself – plenty of biking these days if you can call pushing a collection of weighty old scrap iron around 'biking'.

Food here is still really good and everything apart from no definite time off is OK really. Having no definite time off is a hell of a nuisance – not even half a day off a week for shopping. Best you can hope for is the chance to get off either flying or ground stuff early enough to get into Carlisle to have a meal out for a change and see a cinema.

Have been out of camp only twice since Chris was here and the last time (last night) was a complete wash-out. But when I know there's the possibility of seeing Chris again soon then I don't mind that very much and of course I'm very lucky compared with many fellows…

CROSBY-ON-EDEN
CARLISLE

Friday 26th November 1943

Dearest Mum,

…I've been doing a lot of thinking lately and it all amounts to the fact that now I'm engaged I can't find any pleasure when I'm either not home or when Chris isn't here. I am a dead loss to my pals as I haven't the slightest interest in dances, other girls or drinking. And I'm afraid Mum that I do want to get married soon, whether I stay in England or not. Funnily enough there seems to be a much better chance of staying in England now, I hope so. But if I didn't I'd very much like to get married before I went, and if possible before my leave at the end of this course. Even if it means an upheaval. Of course I can guess that you are absolutely mad at me after reacting this much but I must tell you how I feel, even though it means hurting the feelings of the one person in this world I never will hurt if I can possibly avoid it – you, I mean it and it's not soft soap. I can't explain how I feel about you – you know that as well as I do, and don't think for a moment that if I do get married that my feelings can ever change, and my duties or love can ever alter. I have never written to you like this before, and perhaps should have waited till I can speak

I'm OK myself – doing plenty of biking these days.

to you – it's just that I get so fed up with this waste-of-time sort of existence, and I want to settle things for the future.

I thought at first that if I did go overseas from here for a long time (which could be possible – say two years or more), then I'd like to know that I had a wife to come home to, and to stay interested in me till I got back home, besides having you to come back to. I hope you understand my feelings – I want some definite anchor for the future. Maybe I sound a little cracked, but never mind, forget I mentioned it, though I do want to get married before I go overseas if I go from here, and I'll know that at the end of this course. I believe before I come home on leave.

We'll see – anyway forget it, and don't worry about it, and please forgive me for writing a letter that could have upset you. I'll always be near you and you will share the same place in all I do as well as my wife. I'll not leave it to Ken to look after you, or Pop. I'll be there by your side as though I wasn't married when I get back to civvy street. Chris agrees to, she knows how much I must be with you.

You won't lose me Mum, I'll see to that. The only way you could lose me would be by getting terribly angry with me about wanting to get married so soon and then you could only keep me like that for a little, for I'd just wait for you to forgive me for causing you this extra big anxiety. I'm afraid I'm not explaining myself as I want to but I'll go on and try.

Chris says she will marry me though she doesn't want to upset you about it, and it has been myself that has wanted to get married so soon. I can imagine, only too well, how you're feeling by now after reading this much. You either think I'm mad or have suddenly decided to see how much I can upset you and worry you more than you already are with Ken and I being in the services. And other worries. But I'm not. Chris is the one I want to marry and she is of the same mind, and I can't see any real reason, except this big one of upsetting you Mum, why we shouldn't get married soon, as we wouldn't marry blind.

Don't think this is a sudden blind impulse of mine. It's not. Ever since I've been back in England I've wanted to marry her soon, but seeing that it would upset you more than I could stand, or would want to happen as you mean more to me than most fellows seem to think of their mothers, I have said that I'd be satisfied with getting engaged and would probably wait till after the war.

Well I've thought about it a terrible lot, have talked and written a lot to Chris about it, but although it might seem underhand, I had

Having a married son Mum will be no different to an unmarried one – in fact he'd be settled down and more stable.

decided to say nothing about it for a while, because of causing you the worry I know it will.

But you like Chris don't you and she certainly has a great deal of respect and affection for you, (one of the reasons, without exaggerating, why I want her to be my wife), and you won't be losing me one little bit, you'll only be gaining her, and I'll see to it that as far as definite support for later years goes, you will not want one scrap. Of course that goes without saying really, but I know that all mothers think they lose their sons as soon as they're married. But you are not all mothers – you're my mother and a very special and dear one, and this marriage will not be so much as my getting married but a bringing of Chris into the family. You must see that!

She knows only too well how I feel about you – she knows that I don't think of you as an ordinary son thinks of his mother. She knows you stand for much more than that, and I expect she'll be a bit envious at times. But she knows that and is prepared to run all and any risk of marrying me. By being in love with her and wanting to marry her, it doesn't mean that my love and full sense of what I want to repay you for has dwindled, Mum. If she can live with you as she does now, when I'm stationed any distance from home – which is very probable – then things won't be much different to what they are now really. You'll be company for each other, especially when Pop is on night work.

Quite a few of my pals have got married recently, and many of them after only knowing the girl a short time which is madness. Many of them are only twenty and twenty-one years old. Apparently your wife gets 21s 6d government allowance and I will have to make a minimum allowance of 24s 6d which means Chris would get £2 6s a week without any voluntary allowance from me, which would leave me £6 a fortnight as a sergeant. With that, and Chris working, we should be able to save a fair amount to give us a start with a home after the war and there is much more stuff she could get as a wife than remaining single isn't there?

I should still be able to give you a voluntary allotment, I don't want to stop that for many reasons. I could still save something myself, specially if I get promotion which I should soon – another 2/- a day.

Now I expect all this will have been a nasty shock to you Mum and you will be absolutely amazed and shocked with me.

You'll be thinking that I don't care two hoots for your feelings and am just mad to habour feelings of getting married these days: absolutely putting my neck into complications. But I have thought about it and would not go into it with my eyes closed. Please try to understand Mum. When I'm back in civvy street I'll be as near to you as you were to grandmother and nearer if that's possible, and while I'm in the RAF I'll spend all my leaves at home with Chris as well of course. Home's always my first thought – you know that. Only wish I was with you now to explain everything.

Look Mum, I know if Chris and I get married while I'm on aircrew that we're taking a risk and I realise only too acutely all your feelings, particularly as you lost dad and know what it's like, but nothing's going to happen to me or Ken, and one day this war is going to end and Chris and I are going to live 'next door' to you and Pop and Ken (until he marries).

I'm really in love with her and shan't be satisfied till we've married – you have been the same. But as I have said I'll never, I can't of course, ever neglect you for her. And that won't be necessary. All this business of rows between wives and their husband's mothers may be true in some cases, but it wouldn't be in ours. Please believe me. I still want to spend my time at home, but at the same time I want to get married and start planning for the future. Can't it be possible.

Nothing is going to happen to me flying, but if it ever did then the will I'd make if I get married will see that any little benefits as far as money goes will not all go to my next of kin.

I expect you'll think me mad with talk like this, but won't you please make me happy by not being upset about my wanting to marry Chris soon.

I am in two minds whether to send this or not for however lenient you are, I know I will upset you. You don't expect me to think like this so soon I know, but as I have thought so, and very seriously too, I thought I'd better be quite open about it long before I acted. I'll not be happy, in fact I'll be intensely miserable if you go off the deep end, and refuse to say you wouldn't mind so much. You are the only person whose feelings I am badly worried about in this obsession to get married soon, and I know you cannot help but be mad at me. But please say that you wouldn't object terribly Mum, after all we would get married some day, and why not now. What difference would it make?

There's the chance we've heard of four days instead of a '48' soon, and on that time, if I get it, we could arrange things, if you agree. Should be 10th or 17th.

Having a married son would be no different to an unmarried one – in fact he'd be settled down and more stable. I know it means many responsibilities but I'm prepared for that.

So would you mind if we did get married much sooner than everyone expects so very much Mum? Please say 'yes', and what ever you do don't get upset about it, for there's no reason to. As I say, by marrying I'll not be breaking up our family (God forbid) but just bringing Chris into it.

Please Mum!

Wish I were home right now to talk to you about everything I want to, but in two or three weeks time, perhaps before, I'll be home and then we can.

Now I must close. I shrink inside me at the thought of your feelings at first when you read all this but I must say this Mum, I hope and trust that you won't be upset about it.

Forgive me Mum if I've been awkward and hurt your feelings. I'd be happy single if I were in civvy street, and could court Chris a long time, but I don't want the chance of losing her to someone else as might easily happen if I am away from home again a long time. She is a girl in a thousand. So many cases of girls having affairs with other men have I seen in the RAF, and I know she's not like so many others, and I want her for a wife. And not give anyone else a chance.

I could go on all night explaining my reasons for wanting to get married so soon. They are many. But my biggest concern is upsetting you. Otherwise I'd have spoken long before now, and I could go on writing too, all night asking you not to get upset, and thinking that I don't appreciate or care for your feelings at all. I do, as much as I want to get married. So please understand Mum, and don't forget you wouldn't be losing me or all I could do towards your happiness in the future. I'd see to that.

All my love, you know that.

Your ever loving son

X X X X X Bob X X X X X

CROSBY-ON-EDEN
CARLISLE

27th November 1943

Dearest Mum,

I expect by now you have got my last letter — I hope it hasn't upset you. I'm rather sorry I sent it now — I shouldn't have been so hasty.

I don't think there is much chance of more than a '48' around December 10th and we'll be very lucky to get even that as we are behind with flying times due to bad weather. And even then if we had got it the shock of my wanting to marry Chris so soon would have been very unfair of me to you. And I'd like Ken to be home at least when I do get married.

…Well this idea of getting married — I'd like to as soon as possible, but not if it's going to cause you any pain or worry, and although I know you are the best mother possible, I'll bet you are damned annoyed with me at present after that impetuous letter.

Well forget it Mum please – I can't see how it would be possible with any degree of satisfaction to everybody all round to get married this side of xmas, now.

It would be much too rushed, and I want us to have a decent affair, even in war time if possible with time for arrangements, as I realise it's quite a big thing to accomplish. A lot to think of.

If we do get married in war time of course I'd not think of getting any of the large stuff that constitutes a home, but would have to leave it when Chris and I saved up for the various things to start a home after the war…

CROSBY-ON-EDEN
CARLISLE

Wednesday 22nd December 1943

Dear Ken,

Received your letter this morning about your foreign service leave. I tried my utmost to get a '48' but the bastards won't let me go. I saw the wing commander but after a quarter of an hour's argument he said no! The stupid bugger said it wasn't sufficient compassionate ground. He brought up some irrational nonsense about a fellow who hadn't seen his brother for six years – that's not the point is it! They could have let me go. They have only to give me one day as Christmas Day is free and on Christmas Eve I expect we'll parade around like a lot of bloody sheep and do no flying.

It makes me rave. They can keep their services Ken. The longer I'm in it the more I loathe it. Don't think I am 'browned off' but oh kid I'm fed up with this bloody outfit at times like this.

Anyway I've had the bloodiest morning trying to get leave, moaning won't alter that fact. I feel like taking it but they'll be hot on passes at xmas – even on aircrew. I doubt if I'd get as far as home. If you're away a long time don't despair you'll be back one of these fine days with the satisfaction of having done something material and worthwhile. You'll see bags of places you've never seen in civvy street, and you'll come back with a broader outlook. I know you'll look after yourself and have the best of ideas how things should be and your sense of values I know is the best. Believe me I couldn't have tried harder to get leave Ken – I know you believe that – goodbye again and keep writing.

Love Bob

Dearest Mum & Pop,

Please forgive me for not writing to you for these last few days that Chris has been here, but my time was pretty well occupied with the RAF and Chris. I know you'll understand and forgive me, Mum.

Well how are you now? Chris tells me you were expecting old Ken home again at the weekend. I hope he stays near you till the last possible moment before he goes. And he is going to a place where he should have a decent time Mum, so try not to worry over him too much, as you'll make yourself ill, you know.

Damn this war – it brings nothing but heartaches to people. But the news gets better every day doesn't it? The Russians will soon be in Germany at this rate. It shouldn't be too long now. We must be patient I suppose, but as every day goes by I long more and more to be home for good.

Chris makes life so comfortable when she comes up here. She does lots of little odd jobs for me. She's nearly as good as you in this respect. There is nothing more I want now than the chance to settle down with her near you.

I haven't lost interest in flying however, I have been doing pretty well lately. My shooting at air targets and ground strafing seems to be OK so far, and I am rather pleased with myself. I seem to do OK at it and really rather surprised myself as I'm not much good with a rifle on the ground, though I've had little practice. But air firing is totally different. You have to be able to fly a plane without thinking about flying it – automatically really I mean, and concentrate on the target in your sights, and so far I have coped OK.

I was rather dubious and apprehensive at the start of this course. I didn't fancy my chances on fighters, although as you know I've always wanted them. But now I am confident, but still careful – don't worry. The only chances I take are the ones you have to take and they are rare and not dangerous.

I received some stationery and a 12s 6d PO from the firm while Chris was here. They aren't generous but they are reliable and I'll be glad to get back to a settled regular sort of existence working for them. It'll be a start.

Was wondering the other day if they'd allow me anything when I get married – they make an allowance to married men. At least they did at the start of the war when I was there.

Well Mum, must close to catch the afternoon post. Look after yourselves for me, and keep your chin up, Mum, about our Ken. He'll be OK.

All my love, and God bless.

Yours as ever

Bob X X X X X X

CROSBY-ON-EDEN
CARLISLE

10th January 1944

Dearest Mum & Pop,

The news of Chris going into hospital was a shock to me, I must say.

…I know it isn't a very serious operation but naturally I'd like to be home at the moment as much as I wanted to see Ken, and can't help feeling worried. I expect you are very worried too. I am ever so sorry, Mum, that you have this extra worry besides your feelings about our Ken. And I wish I were home to help the little bit I could. I tried yesterday and today to get compassionate leave, but they wouldn't hear of it.

...So if the doctor says OK would you go ahead with the arrangements for the wedding Mum if you possibly can. I'm always asking you to do everything for me, and when ever I want anything it's always you I come to. But believe me, when I'm out of this outfit I'll do my best to repay a little of the years of attention and worry you've spent on me and Ken (I'm the biggest worry – I know). All I can do is put the bans in here. Apparently I must get the station padre to do it here for me before we can get married, but there's no need for them to be read out at home. So that is one little thing removed from your shoulders, if we can manage it Mum.

...If we can get married in February Mum, we must have a very quiet affair. Whether it's a white wedding or not is up to Chris. But the reception will have to be very quiet with only the people there who we really want to come.

Of course I realise that if it is OK for us to get married Chris will have to be very careful for a while and we'll have to forget 'first nights' for a while. I realise all that and you must realise that I know it Mum, won't you?

All I want is for us to get married before I might have to go overseas. I have told you all the reasons why.

I'll bet you think I'm mad to want to get married in view of this 'turn-out', but the doctor says she'll be fit to stand the strain of a wedding ceremony and if you can manage all the arrangements on top of all you have to do already, then I do want us to get married when I finish here...

RAF
NORTH COATES

Friday 20th May 1944

Dearest Mum & Pop,

I've let my letter writing slip, I'm afraid, but Chris wrote two letters so I thought it would be OK to let mine slide for a couple of days.

Well, how are you both; keeping well I hope? I've had two letters from you since I wrote last Mum – thank you, and you say you are both OK. That's good.

Sorry you haven't heard from Ken of late – perhaps you have by now.

I had a pleasant surprise a couple of days ago. John Sullivan sent me a parcel of books; all his folk seem OK.

There was a dance in the mess last night, and I took Chris along. We had a decent time, but my God! there was enough beer around to float a small boat. Anyway we were OK. Some of the fellows look a bit worse for wear this morning tho'.

I don't know if Chris has remembered it, but after this next leave she may not come back here, because I get less and less chance to leave camp of late and I expect it to become practically nil in the future with the possibility of course of being moved too. I think she'll go home to her mother. Apparently her mother has been ill for the last six weeks.

Anyway we're not sure yet, but shall know definitely what we'll do by the time we are home on leave. (A week today it should be).

Well Mum, once again it's only a very short letter, but anyway just another week and I'll be with you again.

Cheerio then and look after yourselves. God bless!

Your loving son
as always

Bob X X X X X X X

There was a dance in the mess last night, and I took Chris along.

30th June 1944

Dearest Mum & Pop,

I've been pretty busy since I got back one way and another and really forgot till the post had gone this morning that I hadn't written. Please forgive me Mum.

We had a decent journey. Had to stand for a little while that's all. Have got settled down in North Coates with Chris. [Bob and Chris were married in February 1944.] Am staying with Mrs Westbrook for a little while – have the chance of a little furnished house quite close, perhaps in a week's time. It's not very much I shouldn't think, but we'll have it to ourselves I hope, and that should be much better.

I hope these damned robot bombs aren't so frequent since we've left. I wish you could leave London till they cease. What do you intend doing with your week's holiday Mum? The Midlands would be out of range of those bombs.

…I'm glad I've taken my bike with me this time as its certainly a great improvement on service bicycles.

I shall write to Ken today I think. Have you heard any more from him. I expect you'll be anxious for a letter from me, and I could kick myself for forgetting.

Well then, cheerio for a little while, look after yourself, (Pop too) and try and not worry too much ay?

Your loving son
as always

Bob X X X X X X X X X

I have been terribly busy ... making up for lost time.

I've been pretty busy since I got back one way and another.

RAF
NORTH COATES

Saturday 15th July 1944

Dearest Mum & Pop,

Once more please forgive me for letting my letter-writing slip. Save for your two letters Mum. Thank you for your letters and thanks for forwarding that bill on too. We sent the money same day I received it, so it'll be OK now. Chris and I had completely forgotten about it.

I have been very busy this last week and haven't seen nearly so much of Chris of late. It is still easily worth while having her here though.

She was very disappointed, and so was I, when we received your letter saying you wouldn't be coming. This little house of ours is becoming quite cosy now. Chris has worked like a Trojan on it – even to the extent of painting even and whitewashing a wall of the scullery.

I've done very little – I have been too busy. She has made it really clean and comfortable now, and she seems much happier there.

I do hope you will come up here when you wish, especially if these damned buzz bombs are getting you down.

Leave has started again, but mine won't be till August 20th, when I should get nine days.

Any more letter from Ken Mum? Well, I must close now. Keep well for me, both of you, won't you and look after yourselves.

Your loving son
as always

Bob X X X X X X X

Chris has worked like a Trojan… even to the extent of painting and whitewashing a wall of the scullery.

RAF NORTH COATES
LINCOLNSHIRE

9th September 1944

Dearest Mum & Pop,

Here I am again making excuses for not writing as often as I should. I received your letter two days ago Mum. Thank you for it too. Chris wrote to you. Hope you received it OK.

I have been terribly busy since I have been back: making up for lost time.

Well Mum and Pop – how are you keeping, well I hope. I hope too that the damned buzz bombs have petered out a great deal. Things are still going well for us with the second front aren't they? In a month or two from now there's every hope of the end of it. And Japan shouldn't take very long after that. I received a letter from J.D. today and a 7s 6d postal order. We have been very lucky there – no serious casualties!

...I should be on leave again about October the 9th – about a month from now.

...Well Mum, that's about all the news for now. I do hope you are keeping well, and Pop too, and not worrying.

Very soon now it seems this damned war will be over and that'll be our biggest worries and fears gone. So hold on a little longer Mum, and we'll make things worth while once again.

Look after yourselves then.

All my love
your loving son

Bob X X X X X X

I hope too that the damned buzz bombs have petered out… In a month or two from now there's every hope of an end to it.

CONVOY DAMAGED BY BEAUFIGHTERS

Beaufighters of R.A.F. Coastal Command, escorted by Mustangs of a Polish squadron of A.D.G.B., attacked with rocket projectiles and cannon fire a formation of enemy naval auxiliary vessels off the Frisian Islands on Sunday evening. Explosions occurred on two of the vessels, one of which probably sank. A third vessel was set on fire, and two others were damaged by cannon fire. One Beaufighter is missing.

News report from the *Daily Telegraph* 12 September 1944.

TELEPHONE: GERRARD 9234
Extn..............

Any communications on the subject of this letter should be addressed to :—
THE
UNDER SECRETARY
OF STATE,
and the following number quoted :— P.422892/1/P.4.B.6.

Your Ref. ....

AIR MINISTRY

(Casualty Branch),

73-77, OXFORD STREET,

W.1

8th August, 1945.

Madam,

I am directed to inform you, with regret, that in view of the lapse of time and the absence of any further news regarding your son, Flight Sergeant A.J. Kimberley, since he was reported missing, action has now been taken to presume, for official purposes, that he lost his life on the 10th September, 1944.

In conveying this information, I am to express to you the sympathy of the Air Ministry.

I am, Madam,
Your obedient Servant,

RaRandall

for Director of Personal Services.

Mrs. H.R. Thurman,
8, Brocklands Gardens,
Hornchurch,
Essex.

Letter from the Air Ministry confirming
that Bob Kimberley had been killed in action.

Honestly, I'd sooner be at home, than in Heaven, if there is such a place!

ACKNOWLEDGEMENTS

I would like to thank my wife, Joan for her constant help and support, for without her *Home Sweet Home* would never have come to fruition. My special thanks to Chris and John for their devotion to my mother over the years. Likewise to all Bob's friends, particularly those mentioned in the letters. My thanks to the very special role they played. My gratitude to the people at the RAF Museum at Hendon for their support and willingness to accept Bob's letters for their historic archives. Finally my grateful thanks to Richard Webb and all at Webb & Bower, to editor Alyson Gregory and designer Vic Giolitto for their advice, enthusiasm and above all their belief in what for me was a very personal undertaking.

Jacket front: RAF insignia. Crown copyright. Reproduced by permission of the Controller of Her Majesty's Stationery Office.

History of RAF North Coates, pages 9–11, reproduced by kind permission of Patrick Stephens Limited, Denington Estate, Wellingborough, Northants.

Ken Kimberley's illustrations are not intended to be exact representations of the uniforms, vehicles, etc. of the era. He regrets any historical inaccuracies.